I'm Black When I'm Singing, I'm Blue When I Ain't
and Other Plays

I'm

Black

W'ner

Sing-

ing

I'm

I'm Black When I'm Singing, I'm Blue When I Ain't
and Other Plays

SONIA SANCHEZ

Edited and with
an Introduction by
Jacqueline Wood

Duke University Press
Durham and London
2010

For H.S., who has been my inspiration,

strength, and comfort always in this journey

and

For Geneviéve Madelaine, whose dedication,

example, and faith in me have made this possible.

Contents

Introduction   xi

Part I. Essays

Poetry Run Loose: Breaking the Rules
(2004)   3

Ruminations/Reflections (1984)   15

Preface to *Uh, Uh; But How Do It Free Us?*
(1974)   19

Part II. Plays

The Bronx Is Next (1968)   25

Sister Son/ji (1969)   36

Dirty Hearts (1971)   44

Malcolm/Man Don't Live Here No Mo
(1972)   53

Uh, Uh; But How Do It Free Us? (1974)   59

I'm Black When I'm Singing, I'm Blue
When I Ain't (1982)   99

2 X 2 (2009)   126

Selected Bibliography   139

Acknowledgments

Many have helped me produce this work. First I must thank Sister Sonia Sanchez for sharing her artistic gifts with the world. I also thank her for her patience and generosity as together we went through the inevitable snags that preparing any book entails. I must express my gratitude to Ken Wissoker for his enthusiastic interest and his kind guidance. I thank Dr. Jane Davis and Dr. Dellita Martin-Ogunsola for their sound advice, their unfailing professionalism, and their loyal friendships. I must acknowledge the University of Alabama at Birmingham and its Minority Faculty and Student Development Program (MFSDP) grant project for enabling me to have time to work on the book. I thank, in particular, Deanna Robertson for her hard work in preparing the word processed draft. I appreciate also the careful readings of that highly intelligent, yet humble, housewife in Ohio who has never failed me yet. I thank Jae, Cha Cha, Mei, and Kye for their priceless contributions in sustaining my spirit. G.I.G.!

—Jacqueline Wood

Introduction:
The Power Plays of Sonia Sanchez

Known for her work as a major poet, teacher, and champion of and for black culture, Sonia Sanchez is regarded worldwide as a living legend, a revered female writer of the black community. This reception is significant in both political and literary domains because, as Joyce Ann Joyce observes in *Ijala*, Sanchez's literary project evinces African tradition where "griots/poets, functioning as guides, teachers, and historians for their respective cultures, embrace their people" (12). Sanchez herself characterizes the African American poet as "a creator of social values," claiming that "the most fundamental truth to be told in any art form, as far as Blacks are concerned, is that America is killing us. But we continue to live and love and struggle and win" ("Ruminations," 16).[1] She explains her own artistic pursuits as drawing on "any experience or image to clarify and magnify this truth for those who must ultimately be about changing the world. . . . The more I learn, the clearer my view of the world becomes. To gain that clarity . . . I had to wash my ego in the needs/aspiration of my people" ("Ruminations," 16, 17). Sanchez has throughout her career attempted both to engage her audience and to examine a writer's responsibilities. In the process, she has become an acclaimed poet/dramatist and civil rights activist, receiving numerous national awards. She has published over sixteen books of poetry, five plays, and several pieces of fiction. Among her most acclaimed poetry collections are *Homecoming* (1969), *We a BaddDDD People* (1970), *Homegirls and Handgrenades* (1984), *Under a Soprano Sky* (1987), *Does Your House Have Lions?* (1997), and *Shake Loose My Skin* (1999).[2] An editor of two anthologies, *We Be Word Sorcerers* (1973) and *Three Hundred and Sixty Degrees of Blackness Coming at You* (1973), Sanchez has also lectured in more than five hundred venues around the world. For her poetry, she has received, among others, the American Book Award, the Robert Frost Medal, and the Patricia Lucretia Mott Award.[3]

Numerous critical discussions have examined how through her poetry collections Sanchez has for over three decades successfully created a forceful artistic stance.[4] However, criticism has not stressed enough that Sanchez has done the same in her dramatic works, which are also poetic and, at least in part, vehicles for poetry. Incorporating the responsibility of the poet into the venue of dramatic art, she has successfully accomplished what few militant writers have done well—transcending the genre divide.

Throughout the 1960s and 1970s, Sanchez achieved notoriety writing poetry and drama as part of the Black Arts movement. Ed Bullins, recognizing the impact of her publications as a militant poet, commissioned Sanchez's first play, *The Bronx Is Next* (1968), for his first edition of *New Plays from the Black Theatre*. Subsequent plays were published in numerous journals and anthologies, including *Sister Son/ji* (1969) in *New Plays from the Black Theatre*; *Dirty Hearts* (1971) in *Breakout*; *Malcolm/Man Don't Live Here No Mo* (1972) in *Black Theater*; and *Uh, Uh; But How Do It Free Us?* (1974) in *New Lafayette Theatre Presents*. These dramatic works exemplify the political protest conventions of black revolutionary drama, a drama that focused on politico/cultural consciousness-raising and, ultimately, demanded change for the African American community,[5] change to be initiated by that community.[6] Black revolutionary drama adopted a rhetoric that emphasized the development of unity in the collective or communal experiences of oppressed black people, in essence politicizing audiences.[7]

However, in spite of creating political and formal conventions that privilege the role and potential of activist communities, the predominantly male circle of black revolutionary dramatists, Sanchez's contemporaries, ultimately limited to some extent in their capacity to effectively represent the black communal experience. Their efforts were hampered by their insistence on a chauvinistic, at times homophobic, rhetorical discourse. Because radicalism in black arts of the 1960s and 1970s was frequently equated with manhood, militant precepts were often expressed through masculinist language. For example, Ed Bullins characterizes the purpose of the black playwright with gendered language: "It is to do the best he can at his job of writing and presenting his vision and not become prematurely emasculated by the prospect of not being produced because of his race" ("Theatre of Reality," 61). Amiri Baraka reveals a similar male-centered stance: "The first thing a writer wants to do is write. . . . (Though this is not at all true, finally, when you look up and find yourself straddling a lady, or foot up on a bar rail. But ideally the writing would be the thing for writers)" ("Black Writing," 161–62). In terms of political motivation, Baraka also observes that "manhood is deemed the ability to oppress by the white man. At least one is more of a man in the sense of being self-sufficient, able to provide for yourself and your family. The last words . . . spoken by a black soldier after his wife is outraged by white men is, simply, 'I ain't no man.' That is, I cannot provide or protect" ("American Sexual Reference," 218). Centering these experiences as cause for black men's bravado in the face of a continued sense of inadequacy and disempowerment, Baraka situates oppression of black men as the overarching concern of the revolutionary movement. Manhood then becomes the accepted, promoted metaphor for freedom and equality in this discourse.

By challenging such male-centered perspectives among many of her militant counterparts, Sanchez made her mark early as she condemned their discourse and the concomitant behaviors she witnessed in the movement. These seemed to her to weaken the viability and productivity of the black community.[8] There is for the most part, however, no historical indication that Sanchez's critiques of the movement were seriously entertained at the time by the men in the community to whom those criticisms were directed.[9] Still, this is where she, as a voice from within a small yet visible group of black female writers of the period, distinguishes herself among authors raising women's concerns in the movement. Sanchez demonstrates, as do several of her female contemporaries,[10] a fresh ability to address self-consciously the problematic language and practices within the black militant community. But her singularity exists in that, while creating militant poetry and essays, she also aggressively emphasized militant dramatic art. Most black militant women writers of the sixties and seventies were poets or essayists or dramatists but were not directly associated with the militant playwrights' community. Sanchez raised her strong voice from among these women by privileging drama in addition to other genres in her artistic vision. As militant dramatists and revolutionaries have done worldwide, she demonstrated here her confidence in the special capacity of drama to evoke revolutionary political change.[11] Baraka explains this notion that drama, in this case black drama, is truly the most immediate literary means for effecting political change. He observes that theater as an art form is "the closest to life. . . . In my work I intend to instruct, inform—educate people so that they will be then able to transform society" (quoted in Bigsby, 135). By including drama in her project, Sanchez, like Baraka, comfortably crossed literary genres in her effort to express the struggles and goals of the black community. She thus had much in common with the predominantly male Black Arts playwrights, who emphasized drama as central to their revolutionary expression because of its accessibility to the masses. Sanchez points out, "We [black militant playwrights] recognized and realized that it was necessary to move the African American, this African, back on the human stage because he/she had been taken off that stage" ("Poetry Run Loose," 9).

In an analysis of the aesthetics of black drama, Kimberly Benston suggests that militant playwrights believed "in political terms . . . when skillfully employed, theatre can become a powerful weapon for the regulation of communal values or, conversely, for radical change. Unlike literature, it makes no demands on its audience of literacy or privacy" (63). Sanchez's emphasis on these qualities of drama is one major reason why she, unlike many of her female counterparts, was embraced by militant male authors. They recognized her ability and interest in writing political drama, an effect that culminated in her relative acceptance within the circle of black male militants like Baraka, Neal, and Bullins. Sanchez observes that "it was the playwriting that I think made me different from the other women writers and linked me with the men" (personal interview, March 5, 2005).[12]

The majority of Sonia Sanchez's plays were written during the 1960s and 1970s. Her first play, *The Bronx Is Next*, was produced in October 1970 by Theatre Black with the University of the Streets in New York City. No formal reviews or production information about this performance are evident. According to Sanchez, the paucity of information concerning early productions such as *The Bronx Is Next* in the community is indicative of the political and social climate of the period. The theater models in the black community during the volatile atmosphere of the 1960s and 1970s were not at all reflective of the stable, predictable, traditional elements of theater commonly conceptualized. Writers in black communities, especially dramatists, were working in a setting that was localized and immediate. In the sixties, unrest literally exploded from within communities. Rebellions—in response to racialized anger, poverty, lack of opportunity, racial violence, and radicalized organization—were rife, and the scene of community theater reflected this atmosphere.[13]

Thus black drama of this period was not written in the context of traditional production nor was it intended for commodified consumption. Militant playwrights were in effect working to bolster the political engagement and development of local communities; they were not producing plays to be reviewed by theater critics in the major media. In fact, they shunned and attempted to undermine the commercialized aspects of the traditional theater apparatus. Thus the construct of radical theater of this period was organic. Often workshopped, productions were at times ephemeral and spontaneous, and performances occurred on street corners, in school auditoriums, in libraries, on university campuses—venues that were not conducive to consistent, professional reviews from the press, black or white. Only highly visible black productions backed by major institutional entities like Joseph Papp's Public Theater saw substantial and consistent review in the press or careful preservation of playbills and production information. The black press did not provide consistent reviews of black theatrical events either. Journals often only briefly acknowledged theater activity in the black community. For example, *Black World* (formerly *Negro Digest*) dedicated one issue a year to a collection of critical essays about black drama and a brief description of theater events and productions across the nation. Even extremely visible black newspapers such as the *Amsterdam News* and the *City Sun* in New York were centered on local news events and social information; they offered limited commentary on cultural or theatrical events that involved black artists in the city. As James Hatch observes in his "Appendix: Theatre Scholarship 2002" in *A History of African American Theatre*, the *Amsterdam News* provided only a weekly "half page of current black performances and shows" (486). Hatch goes on to conclude that "many of . . . [the theatre issues] were funded more by enthusiasm than planning; consequently publications often disappeared after one or two issues" (486).[14]

The production history of Sanchez's plays is indicative of this mercurial production/review environment for black militant drama in the sixties and seventies. Sanchez describes some of her early productions as off-off Broadway in underground theaters or in college environments, often advertised only by flyers. She remembers few, if any, representatives of newspapers present at performances (personal interview, March 5, 2005). *The Bronx Is Next* was never commercially produced, but it still did gain political significance in the black community through the University of the Streets productions and its first appearance in print in the *Drama Review*.[15] The play was later reprinted in *New Plays from the Black Theatre* and *Cavalcade*. Sanchez's second play, *Dirty Hearts*, was never produced, appearing in print first in the New York Shakespeare Festival's *Scripts* (1971). A reprint of the play appeared in *Breakout! In Search of New Theatrical Environments* in 1973. *Malcolm/Man Don't Live Here No Mo*, a commissioned children's play for the Liberation School of Pittsburgh, was produced by Philadelphia's ASCOM Community Theatre in 1979. As this was a small community-based venue, no formal reviews or production information exists for this performance. The play first appeared in print in *Black Theatre: A Periodical of the Black Theatre Movement* in 1972.

Sister Son/ji was Sanchez's most substantially produced and reviewed play. The piece was first produced in 1972 as part of a quartet of plays titled *Black Visions* at Joseph Papp's Public Theater in New York City. Novella Nelson directed the play, with Gloria Foster as performer. Reviews of *Sister Son/ji* appeared in the *New York Post*, *The Nation*, *The New York Times*, *Women's Wear Daily*, *Newsweek*, *The New Yorker*, and others. However, no reviews in local black newspapers seem to have been preserved. The reception for this play in the New York mainstream theatrical climate was somewhat positive. Clive Barnes of *The New York Times* deemed *Sister Son/ji* the "best acted" of the four plays produced but described the content as "self-indulgent," and of "marginal literary interest." Barnes did concede that Sanchez "has a fascinating mind" and that at times her "insights on the growth of a black intellectual are most rewarding." But he concluded that the play, "despite the eloquence of Miss Foster, never becomes theater" (1). Jack Kroll of *Newsweek* saw *Sister Son/ji* as "the weakest of the plays, precisely because it doesn't take advantage of the real behavior of real people in real situations" (93). On the other hand, Walter Kerr in *The New York Times* described the piece as a "breathtaking" monologue "filled with shifting images, jarred rhythms, prancing angers and embarrassments and defiances." In his review, Kerr emphasized the power of Gloria Foster's performance, describing the impact of her work as causing the "tiny stage" to "yield as to a cracked whip" (11:3:1). Other venues for *Sister Son/ji* included a production by Sudan Arts, Southwest, in Houston in 1972; a production at the State University of New York, Buffalo, in 1972; a production at Amherst College in 1974; a production by Jomandi Productions in Atlanta in 1979; a Vinnie Burrows production in 1993 in New York; and a Jolivette Anderson production at the New Stage Theatre in 1994 in Mississippi. The play first saw print in Bullins's *New Plays from the Black Theatre* in 1969. It was reprinted in Elizabeth Brown-Guillory's *Wines in the Wilderness* in 1990.

Uh, Uh; But How Do It Free Us? was not produced but was published in Ed Bullins's *The New Lafayette Theatre Presents*. The play is prefaced in Bullins's anthology with a brief essay of the same name by Sanchez (the third essay offered in this volume). A contemporary literary review of this play appeared in the April 1975 issue of *Black World*. In a positive analysis of this work, Hilda McElroy described Sanchez as a "playwright/visionary" who "attempts to raise the levels of conscious-ness so that Black people (particularly Black women) can free them-selves" (81). She wrote of the play that it successfully projects "ideolo-gies on stage for Black people" and examines "certain relationships between Black woman/Black male in struggle for liberation" (80).

Never before published, *I'm Black When I'm Singing, I'm Blue When I Ain't* saw professional production only once, in 1982. The play was writ-ten for and produced by Jomandi Productions in Atlanta. Directed by Tom Jones, the production boasted Khalil Rahman as musical director and composer, Ron Frazier as choreographer, and Marsha A. Jackson as main actor. *The Atlanta Constitution* favorably reviewed the production. Helene C. Smith described the play as "a strong, somewhat oblique, heavy work . . . that wrings out both audience and cast . . . I didn't understand all of this show with my mind, but I felt every bit of it. And that's no small praise . . . it is strongly worth seeing." *The Atlanta Consti-tution* ran in the same issue a separate article on Sanchez, "Joy and Pain of Writing the Blues," also by Smith. Sanchez was quoted describing her process of writing this play as a commitment to regional theater: "I told them I would write a play for them. . . . Besides, I really would like to help secure them as a company." Smith describes the Jomandi theater as fortunate to "score this coup of being the first to produce a new play by Sanchez" (B:1).

One conclusion that can be drawn from such a spotty production history is that—as with the works of several of her female contempo-raries like Martie Charles, Pearl Cleage, Aisha Rahman, or J. E. Franklin—Sanchez's dramatic work as a whole was diminished in importance if not outright ignored by the mainstream theater scene during the mili-tant period. This was in part because female playwrights were often not taken seriously. When black women playwrights of the period are researched in comparison to male militant playwrights such as Amiri Baraka, Ed Bullins, or Ron Milner, we find that the men, in spite of their political intent and the volatile nature of their drama, were much more recognized and embraced by the traditional theater scene. Admittedly, a good number of the female playwrights were less prolific in their playwriting than Baraka or Bullins. Even so, most wrote at least three or more plays, yet few of these women were consistently produced or considered by critics.[16] Of these women playwrights, Sanchez, with five plays, was the most bold and most prolific professedly militant female dramatist of the time. Yet, or again perhaps because of this uniqueness, only one of Sanchez's plays out of five, *Sister Son/ji*, saw a noticeable amount of production or review. However, alongside her male counterparts, Sanchez continued the battle for attention and engagement of her audiences. She demonstrated that militancy in drama was still considered one of the most potent strategies for addressing the continued assaults on the rights and liberties of African Americans during the mid-twentieth century. These strategies were directed toward a chronic despair resulting from periods in American history fraught with violent racial conflict. A brief look at this history can serve to situate Sanchez's unique role within the revolutionary dramatists' movement.

Historical Context

In the early 1950s, intense racism still gripped America. Vigorous implementation of the Black Codes of the early-twentieth-century had entrenched in whites the notion of segregation as an acceptable social approach in American life, both in the North and the South.[17] The coming of war, however, had offered opportunity for African Americans to prove their patriotism and serve their country. Yet the brave service of black men and women during the two world wars did not substantively alter prospects for African Americans. Many had hoped that fighting for freedom overseas would prove their worth as American citizens and earn them equality at home. In the years following the Second World War, however, little changed in terms of racist social and political behavior in America. Increasingly stringent "separate-but-equal" policies in both the North and South were assuredly separate yet anything but equal, still promulgating the Jim Crow realities of African American experience. Segregation had been and continued to be the calculated outcome of ongoing racial violence, most evidenced through lynchings, race riots, and mob attacks. Legalized discrimination laws derived primarily from the *Plessy v. Ferguson* (1896) court case further buttressed segregationist policies, and these policies persisted as the central formulation of almost every social reality for blacks and whites.[18] Such prejudice continually forced blacks into a chronically inferior position defined by "colored-only" water fountains and public facilities, poor access and limited comfort in public transportation and housing. There also continued unequal disbursement of educational opportunity, due process, and substantive political rights.

For example, segregation in public grade schools fostered an ever-increasing gap between a black child's and white child's educational opportunities. The average expenditure per black pupil in at least ten southern states in 1910 was $2.90 whereas for white children the per capita was $9.45. These states included Alabama, Arkansas, Florida, Georgia, Louisiana, Mississippi, and South Carolina. By the middle of the next decade the outlay per black child had dropped to $2.89 while outlays for each white child had increased to $10.32 (Kluger 109, 165). By 1930, in Maryland, North Carolina, Virginia, Texas, and Oklahoma allocations for education of whites were twice those for blacks (168). In Florida and Georgia, white children received five times as much funding as black children, while ten times as much funding was provided for a white child as for a black child in South Carolina. In essence, this trend of separate and unequal funding, rather than showing any possibility of subsiding, actually evidenced a clear escalation of inequality. According to Charles Houston, special counsel to the NAACP, in 1932–33 in South Carolina, the state expended over $331,000 on transportation for 29,624 white students yet only $628.00 to transport 87 black students (Kluger, 205). By the 1950s, segregation and unequal access to government funding were still absolute in southern public schools (Klarman, 291). For the average black in the South, this meant that children could attend only black schools, where they experienced inferior, often outdated and damaged textbooks, poorly paid teachers, and small, dilapidated school buildings in remote or nearly inaccessible places.[19]

In addition, black children often could only haphazardly tend to their education because of their need to work to supplement parental income. Parents worked long hours at low-paying jobs primarily in agricultural or industrial settings—in mills, on large white-owned farms, or scraping out a living sharecropping. Black entrepreneurship, attempts at political office, even pursuit of the vote were discouraged through violence and intimidation. Lynching was by far the most effective and immediate deterrent to black progress. This act of violent killing involved mobs from three to thousands of individuals who attacked defenseless blacks by beating, mutilating, torching, and often hanging living victims. Lynching was used as a white form of terrorism—spuriously justified at first as a device to keep order and later supposedly to protect the sexual safety of white women. Between the years 1882 and 1968 over 3,400 blacks were lynched, with more than half of these murders occurring in the twentieth century ("U.S. Lynchings," 3). As a result, black poverty and despair festered in the wake of Jim Crow policies.

Disenfranchisement served to further enable such abuse. With no voice in government decisions and public policy, African Americans had no recourse by which to address the abuses of their rights. As a result, voting continued to be a central issue in attempts toward black progress. Efforts to register black voters in the South were continuously foiled by inequitable poll taxes, literacy tests, grandfather clauses, misleading primary votes, and outright intimidation. Violent acts of the Ku Klux Klan—which by the 1930s boasted of over five million members—and like groups forced prospective registrants into hiding and wrought havoc in the lives of black citizens attempting to be heard at the polls. According to the Southern Regional Council, only 2 percent of all eligible blacks of voting age in 1940 were actually qualified to vote in twelve states in the South. By 1952 this figure had quadrupled in upper southern states like West Virginia and Kentucky. However, in the Deep South no visible improvement in the qualification of black voters was permitted within this twelve-year period (Woodward, 142–43). In addition, after 1954 the small progress toward black voter qualification in the South began to wane as southern resistance to desegregation began to build.

These were the problems that the Truman administration made attempts to address through such measures as the Committee on Civil Rights in 1947, the Fair Economics Practice Commission in 1948, and the deliberate desegregation of the military (Woodward, 136). However, the subsequent Eisenhower administration stalled Truman's efforts. Eisenhower's laissez-faire attitude allowed southern resistance toward desegregation and racist southern policies to flourish (Woodward, 138). As a result, in response to continued relegation of blacks to second-class status, issues of race during these decades continued to escalate, to be openly contentious and exacerbated by the relatively accommodationist and primarily unsuccessful pursuit of integration by the general black population in the 1940s and 1950s.

The NAACP, however, consistently applied pressure through litigation against Jim Crow practices, eventually effecting a major shift in the fortunes of black progress. A groundswell toward activism began to build after the NAACP's courageous efforts ultimately won audience with the U.S. Supreme Court. The judicial branch of the federal government finally took action to address policies of segregation and to rectify the proliferation of black oppression via Jim Crow ideology. With the outcome of the groundbreaking Supreme Court decision *Brown v. Board of Education of Topeka* in 1954, which outlawed segregation, blacks began more forcefully to address social opportunities and challenge oppression.[20] African Americans worked to openly confront Jim Crow policies. Sit-ins, freedom rides, voter's rights movements, and lawsuits grew in importance as successful ways of challenging and overturning racist systems in America. By the middle of the 1960s, African Americans had begun to create through the civil rights movement a frank, visible, organized response to the unacceptable conditions of their political and social lives in the United States.

It is within this context of political awareness and activism that the Black Arts movement aligned itself with the Black Power movement, working as a venue for burgeoning militant philosophies. The main objective of the Black Power movement was to openly and actively challenge racial oppression in America. This political force was inspired and informed by the writings and activism of black militants such as Huey P. Newton (co-founder with Bobby Seale of the Black Panther Party of Self Defense),[21] Stokely Carmichael (chairman in 1966 of Student Nonviolent Coordinating Committee [SNCC] and in 1968–69 prime minister of the Black Panther Party),[22] Angela Davis, Ericka Huggins, Eldridge Cleaver, and Malauna Karenga, among others. The movement adopted the position that African Americans were a colonized people, a stance founded on American black nationalists' growing alignment with the experiences and voices of oppressed blacks around the world.[23] The movement also emphasized the celebration of black American humanity and identity and, with that, black self-determination (black consciousness). The Black Power movement advocated and facilitated organized communal activism that would determinedly work toward, as Stokely Carmichael argued in 1966, "a new society. . . . Racism must die, and the economic exploitation of non-white people around the world, must also die" ("Black Power," 462). And as Huey Newton declared in 1968 while he was minister of defense of the Black Panther Party, the quest was for "power to determine the destiny of our black community" ("Huey Newton Talks," 491). These premises of the Black Power movement provided the Black Arts movement with direct support and inspiration for its creative expression. The Black Power movement also encouraged an awareness of communal audience, an approach that the Black Arts movement addressed and developed primarily through the genres of poetry and theater—as these genres were most closely tied to the community by oral and performance traditions. Such traditions approached audiences directly during collective experiences at performance events and were thus accessible to all strata of the community. The movement could and did create as a result an art aesthetics that reflexively engaged its political content.

The Black Arts movement insisted on texts and performances that encompassed an ethics of black political commitment. These texts were specifically designed to shock, to challenge, to reject and undermine traditional forms and traditional reception of the poetic and theater arts that transmitted the politics of the dominant culture. As an alternative, black poetry and drama embraced and developed black rhetorical devices to elicit audience consciousness and activism. Some of these devices—often ritualized through an acceptance and reiteration of African art precepts—included allegorical or abstract characterizations; hyperbole; stylized, rhythmic language; poetic litany; colloquialism; idiom; inconsistent semantics; and signification.[24] In addition, the black revolutionary play often used episodic melodrama and open endings, thus moving away from linear structures and traditional emphasis on verisimilitude.

In terms of themes, in early black literature at the turn of the century, dramatic theorists and playwrights, while expressing themselves in relatively traditional forms of language and idea, still focused on black resistance to stereotypes, economic oppression, and racial violence such as lynching. For playwrights/theorists of the sixties, however, resistance themes became more revolutionary in tone; dramatic works evolved into a theater of agitation and propaganda, reflecting the movement's reach toward new forms of expression for black resistance. Black agitprop theater proposed violent, didactic tenets aimed at a politics of communal awareness and solidarity. Theorists such as Ron Milner and Amiri Baraka expressed the nationalist, revolutionary, and polemical bent of black theater and its views concerning the potential of audience reception and participation, views that Sanchez also demonstrates in her theory and plays. Moving away from traditional views of black theater that centered on "appeals to *share* [elements of] power," new black playwrights worked to recognize audience/community as the essential ingredient of black political and artistic revolt. They worked toward an agitprop drama that glorified "*seizures* of power" (Hay, 96; my emphasis).

Literary Significance

In terms of drama, Sonia Sanchez is generally pigeonholed today as a typical black militant playwright of the 1960s and 1970s. However, Sanchez actually created an original voice in her early drama and through each succeeding play transcended black militancy, moving toward a more global, intercultural pursuit of justice. Sanchez's plays certainly address and at times embrace black male prescriptions for militant dramatic propaganda and literary conventions. But she is also true to a specific vision in that her drama reaches beyond the restrictive notions of black nationalist dogma of the militant period. While embracing the valuable work and elements of the militant movement, she introduced to the genre a refreshingly self-conscious look at the negative formulations of black militant practice—its hedonism, its hypocrisy, and its forms of bigotry. In particular, Sanchez condemns the racism and sexism that she encountered as a young female writer within the black militant community and then works toward a larger perspective that demands the destruction of oppression as it affects women, other races, and other cultures.

The Bronx Is Next, Sanchez's first published play, demonstrates elements representative of her revolutionary plays and dramatizes militant themes. Here Sanchez portrays poverty and the smoldering anger of urban black communities through her characterization of militant figures and fiercely realistic street language and behavior. The play examines the complexity of community response to revolution, focusing on a growing sense of futility and anger demonstrated by the local militants' plans to destroy their own Harlem neighborhoods. At the same time, the text presents a concomitant fear of displacement and loss expressed in some residents' refusal to participate in the plan or to leave their homes voluntarily. As the militant characters speak of "burning out the ghettoes," there still is one who exclaims, "Don't make much sense to me man. But orders is orders" (35). The play continues a trend, for it reflects the same issues that Sanchez's poetry had begun to examine. For example, a related radicalism is evident in Sanchez's first published book of poetry, *Homecoming* (1969). One of her most searing early poems in this collection, "for unborn malcolms," parallels the seething anger toward the white oppressor festering within the black community that is depicted in *The Bronx Is Next*. The poem reads in part, "git the word out . . . / . . . that . . . / the next time he kills one / of our/blk/princes. . . . / . . . the main course / is gonna be his white meat. / yeah" (28). The tone in these lines is similar to that of the play.

In exposing the power of communal emotions and consequent militant activism, Sanchez also demonstrates in *The Bronx Is Next* her courage in recognizing and portraying the weaknesses within the black community, in this case by foregrounding some male activists' harsh views of the community. She is thus able to overcome the strong in-fluence of her peers and broaden the thematic thrust of her drama beyond typical militant subject matter and rhetoric even this early in her literary career. From this stance, the play self-consciously ex-amines intra-racial chauvinism in the black militant community by exposing the young male characters as manifesting contempt for the common people. In a moment of frustration, for example, one mili-tant, Charles, observes about his own community members in Harlem, "It's hard working with these people. They like cattle you know. Don't really understand anything" (28). This critique of militant insensitivity toward the community is also evident in excerpts of Sanchez's title poem in the collection *Homecoming*: "once after college / i returned tourist / style to watch all / the niggers killing / themselves. . . . / i have learned it / ain't like they say / in the newspapers" (9). Sanchez's hon-est critique of corrupted weakness within the community also attacks the complacent, intellectualized distance that many educated blacks exhibited in response to the struggles in impoverished, drug-infested black neighborhoods.

The Bronx Is Next also establishes a complex literary voice for the black woman's experience. Reverberations in style occur across two genres here as articulations of poetic language emerging in both Sanchez's drama and poetry. For example, in the play a central female character is rendered powerless, relegated to mere stereotype. The black male militants address her by the only name she has in the play, Black Bitch. She expresses her distress and her call for black male self-awareness in the most poetic sequence of this play:

> Yeah, I know all about black men. The toms and the revolutionary ones. . . . [But] . . . My kids . . . Two beautiful black boys. Smart boys you hear? . . . They will know what a woman is for. . . . I ain't edu-cated, but I'll say—hold them in your arms—love them—love your black woman always. I'll say I am a black woman and I cry in the night. . . . Yeah. I know what I am. . . . But all you revolutionists or nationalists or whatever you call yourselves—do you know where you at? (32)

Sanchez iterates a related cynicism toward black American male be-havior in her poem "summary" in *Homecoming*. A part of the poem reads, "listen. / fool / black / bitch of fantasy. life / is no more than / . . . gents / and / gigolos / (99% american) / liars / and / killers (199% american) dreamers / and drunks (299% / american)" (14). Examples here in drama and poetry demonstrate the sense of anger, frustration, and/or futility that many black women felt concerning male/female relationships.

Suffering and oppression of women are also powerfully revealed in Sanchez's second play, *Sister Son/ji*. One central character delivers a monologue as stylized lyric poetry, further developing Sanchez's tactic of dramatic poetic language briefly introduced in *The Bronx Is Next*. Emphasis on poetry in *Sister Son/ji* also responds to heightened public reception of an increasingly successful expressiveness in Sanchez's poetry collections. *Sister Son/ji* poetically reverences one of the community's wise and aging black mothers, Son/ji, a woman attempting to remember and retrace her past as a way of teaching her listeners about the value of life, of love, of women, and of community. She begins:

> My young days have gone, they passed me by so fast that i didn't even have a chance to see them. What did i do with them? What did i say to them? do i still remember them? Shd i remember them? . . . am i not old? older than the mississippi hills i settled near. Ain't time and i made a truce so that i am time a blk/version of past/ago & now/time. no, if i want to i shall remember. rememberings are for the old. What else is left them? (36–37)

In a dream/memory, she speaks of the militant movement from her perspective as a young college girl,

> no more fucking SIT/ins-toilet/ins-EAT/ins—just like he says—the time for ins is over and the time for outs is here. out of this sadistic/masochistic/society that screams its paleface over the world. the time for blk/nationhood is here. . . . i will talk to sisters abt loving their blk/men and letting them move in tall/straight/lines toward our freedom. (39)

Having looked back at her experiences, she ultimately closes the play through the prism of age and wisdom. She declares:

> Death is a five o'clock door forever changing time. And wars end. Sometimes too late. . . . but i have my memories. *(Rises)* Yes. hee, hee. i have my sweet/astringent memories. . . (43)

Reflections with the same sense of reverence for aged experience and for ancestral wisdom of a guiding mother occur in Sanchez's poem "Kwa mama zetu waliotuzza" ("for our mothers who gave us birth") from the collection *I've Been a Woman* (1978). Published nearly ten years after *Sister Son/ji*, this poem is one of the first to directly reference lines from Sanchez's drama as unequivocal manifestations of cross-genre call/response. Note the initial line of this part of the poem in relation to closing lines from *Sister Son/ji*: "Death is a five o'clock door forever changing time. / . . . and it was morning male in speech; / feminine in memory" (99). This excerpt echoes the imagery and impact of passage of time, memory, and everyday life that Son/ji expresses. Also, in the last lines of *Sister Son/ji*, Son/ji demonstrates Sanchez's revolutionary call for change by challenging the audience to act: "we dared to pick up the day and shake its tail until it became evening. a time for us. blk/ness. blk/people. Anybody can grab the day and make it stop. can u my friends? or maybe it's better if i ask: WILL YOU?" (43). A similar challenge occurs in an excerpt from the poem "blk/rhetoric" from the collection *We a BaddDDD People* (1970): ". . . like who's gonna / take all the young / long / haired / natural / brothers and sisters / and let them / grow til / all that is / impt is them / selves / moving in straight / revolutionary / lines . . . . / this. is an SOS / me. calling . . . . / calling . . . . / some /one / pleasereplysoon" (15–16). In addition to their revolutionary stances, such examples illustrate that poetic structure and personalized content are centrally developed as part of Sanchez's artistic vision in both genres.

Repetition in "Blk/Rhetoric" is also a foreshadowing of the development of litany, a poetic device that Sanchez introduces in her play *Dirty Hearts*, one year after the poetry collection *We a BaddDDD People* was published. Sanchez's choice of litany has a number of political purposes in this play and in future dramatic works. The oral/aural nature of litany as repetitive recitation engages the most fundamental tradition in African American communal life, that of the church. Litany is repetition of lists, verses, phrases, but it also can be a defined series of invocations and responses. Still an element of Catholic and other churches' rituals, litany is also relevant to the oral practices of the historical black church, perhaps most recognizably in the form of call and response. Since oral ritual forms in the black church were and continue to be more fluid than in historically European contexts, Sanchez's use of litany here seems intended to stir the cultural memory of the black audience, soliciting through oral poetic form a communal identification to further black political awareness and activism.

Litany in this third play also demonstrates Sanchez's increasingly distilled use of poetry in drama. Briefly, *Dirty Hearts* is an allegorical presentation of American racial and sexual politics worked out in the dynamics of a card game that dooms the player who receives the most points. Characters in this play turn to intensely lyrical poetic dialogue to emphatically express their deepest emotions. In *Dirty Hearts*, Shigeko, a disfigured victim of the atomic bomb—a Hiroshima maiden—is a main, although disempowered, player in the game.[25] She exposes the wounds of her body and soul in lyrical, ritualized poetic lines excerpted here:

> *(Softly)*
> i have been forgotten by those who once knew me. . . .
> i have been mourning for sterile faces
> i have been obliged. (46)

The strategy of litany evident in *Dirty Hearts* also resurfaces in Sanchez's collection *Love Poems* (1973). In "Poem No. 12" similar repetitious lines occur: "when i am woman, then i shall receive the sun . . . / when i am woman, then I shall give birth to myself . . . / when i am woman . . ." (70). Such formal reiterations further demonstrate Sanchez's sensuous relationship with the written/spoken word in both her poetry and her drama.

Another clear connection between her poetry and drama is manifested in Sanchez's subsequent use of the three *Dirty Hearts* characters—the Poet, Shigeko, and Carl—as personae of poems for a special section titled "3X3" in the poetry collection *Under a Soprano Sky* (1989), published sixteen years after *Dirty Hearts*. In their new venue, the three characters reproduce verbatim their poetic litanies expressed in the play. Only one observable difference occurs: the Poet is characterized as one who "speaks after silence" (35). The import of these dramatic characters' reappearances in a poetry volume seems elusive at first. However, some significance in their reiteration is evident in the trajectory of Sanchez's poetic development, which directly echoes the shifts of vision in her drama. Sanchez's plays began to move away from strident militancy toward a more introspective, personal consciousness and expression of concern for social justice, a progression beginning after *The Bronx Is Next*. While anger toward racial oppression is clearly evident in all of Sanchez's plays, *Dirty Hearts* is more indirect in its language, in its development, and in its representation of revolutionary as well as personal themes and characters. The same kind of shift occurs in the developing trajectory of Sanchez's poetry collections. Where earlier collections like *Homecoming* directly confront with violently angry expression the ills of American race relations, *Under a Soprano Sky* moves away from such strategies, a change signaled in precedent collections like *Love Poems* (1973) or *Blues Book for Blue Black Magical Women* (1974). *Soprano Sky* works with subtle, indirect language and imagery, illuminating a more complex sensibility concerning the implications of oppression. Sanchez thus reintroduces the dramatic characters Poet, Shigeko, and Carl in this collection to depolarize, as *Dirty Hearts* does, images of oppression and aggressive confrontation and to reach toward an increasingly intricate revelation of African American social experience in dramatic and poetic terms.

Finally, thematics in Sanchez's plays *Sister Son/ji* and *Uh, Uh; But How Do It Free Us?* are also iterated in her poetry. Sanchez indicates, in both, an urgent purpose to encourage sensitivity among black men toward their women. The collection *Love Poems*, for example, characterizes the torment black women feel as they survey distressing relationships between black men and women. Lines from "To All Brothers: From All Sisters" illustrate: "who am i to be touched at random? / to be alone so long. to see you move . . . / with the same / shadings of disrespect covering your voice. . ." (95). Much as we will see in *Uh, Uh; But How Do It Free Us?*, her last published play and a very sharp, critical exposition of black male chauvinism, Sanchez reveals in this poem a kind of mourning. She exposes the sad, inescapable consequences of black men's experiences and personal choices. The black man's struggle for identity inevitably impacts his intimacy with, and the well-being of, the black woman, the black family, and, ultimately, the black community.

As these examples demonstrate, the intertextual conversations among Sanchez's poetic and dramatic works illustrate a consistent commitment to community imbued in her artistic purpose. Both drama and poetry demonstrate how her insights broaden and deepen over time. In her art, Sanchez's concerns for the black community and particularly black women become strikingly evident, and her contempt for sexism, racism, and oppression builds force and strength. Sanchez's art thus over time matures and presents a literary voice both unique and valued in the black community.

The Plays

This overview of Sanchez's plays, while brief, still demonstrates her considerable accomplishments in drama and contributions to black literary history. In *The Bronx Is Next*, three characters—black revolutionary figures Charles, Roland, and Jimmy—are forcing tenants into the streets as part of their organization's protest plan to address the horrible conditions of Harlem tenements. The play's conventional use of liberation rhetoric (language with the central purpose of agitating for the freedom of individuals) situates the piece firmly within the militant tradition. Using colloquial language, the text is designed to shock and incorporates frequent, angry condemnations of white power structures and polarized representations of race. For example, Charles, responding to White Cop's flippant reference to the poverty-stricken tenants in Harlem, observes, "Yeah. That's the white man for you man. Always understating things. But since both you and I know that these places are shit-houses, that conversation can end now" (28). Charles continues a little later, "as long as white people hate because of a difference in color, then they ain't gonna let the black man do too much. You dig?" (29). *The Bronx Is Next*'s emphasis is on the merits and difficulties of black activism directly in the face of racism.

Yet the play also self-consciously examines intra-racial chauvinism in the black militant community through its characterization of young militant males. During their interaction with the tenants, the young activists encounter an old woman who adamantly refuses to abandon her special belongings. Illustrating a disregard for the elderly of the community, Charles, in spite of Jimmy's protests, sends her back to her apartment. Charles manipulates the weak, elderly black woman into a building that the activists know will be burned that night. This frightening decision is precipitated by the militants' need to avoid delay of their political program. Although revolution is the single most important thing on their minds, through such an action these men exemplify a callous, paternalistic attitude toward the elderly and particularly toward black women. This attitude is further illustrated by Charles's vicious treatment of a young woman in the community. The revolutionaries confront her, labeling her as Black Bitch in spite of her attempts to prove that her relationship with a white cop is strictly for money to support her children. Charles verbally humiliates and physically abuses the woman while, in contrast, Jimmy attempts to aid her. Ultimately, these two male characters' contrary responses reflect the debate concerning revolutionary commitment as it might contradict individual need. Sanchez characterizes the melding here of youthful compassion, generational conflict, political violence, and sexual bigotry, a combination that blurs perspectives within the revolutionary community. The patriarchal oppression of women and the elderly demonstrated by some members within the Black Power movement is one obviously important concern of this play.

Sanchez's next play, *Sister Son/ji*, employs similar revolutionary thematic strategies and thus also falls within the parameters of black militant drama. Son/ji, reminiscing about her experiences as a young African American woman maturing during the black militant movement, embraces radicalism and declares her loyalty to Malcolm X: "he is not the racist here in white/america. he is a beautiful/blk/man who talks about separation cuz we must move there" (39). However, as well as employing militant liberation rhetoric, *Sister Son/ji* also explores the roles of women—in particular, the vital role of black female college students in the movement. The play suggests that these young women's personal interactions with black men often deteriorated into a mimesis of confrontational male/female relationships within the larger black community. For example, Son/ji's memory-narratives describe the hurtful realization that in a movement fundamentally informed by notions of equality and freedom, young black women were often relegated to disempowered roles as breeders of new warriors or as submissive supporters of their warrior men.

As a young and naive yet strong and determined black female revolutionary, Son/ji eventually comes to terms with her losses resulting from racial and sexual injustice. In a recent interview, Sanchez describes Son/ji's memory events as framed in "meaningful moments" (Wood, 125). As the central construct of the play, these "meaningful moments" reveal Son/ji to us. When we encounter her first as an old woman of wisdom and dignity, reliving her development into womanhood, she presents to us the sexism young black women activists experienced. The character Son/ji also demonstrates that, as a female playwright attempting to personalize community, Sanchez could and would adopt an approach that conflicted with the goals of her black male counterparts. At first, Son/ji is still idealistic: "this morning i heard a sister talk about blk/women supporting their blk/men, listening to their men, sacrificing, working while blk/men take care of bizness, having warriors and young sisters. i shall leave . . . with her words on my lips" (39). However, she is quickly able to perceive the inequities in the movement's role expectations:

> Stay home with me and let us start building true blk/lives—let our family be . . . built on mutual love and respect. . . . blk/people gots

to spend all their spare time together or they'll fall into the same traps their fathers and mothers fell into when they went their separate ways and one called it retaining their manhood while the other called it just plain/don't/care/about/family/hood. (40)

The question of the well-being of black family and male/female relationships is demonstrated as critical here to Sanchez's view of a successful militant movement.

In *Sister Son/ji*, Sanchez refines militant textual approaches that challenge linear plot and emphasize ritualized language. Her structural strategies include reveries and shifts in time sequences to interrupt traditional notions of beginning, middle, and end. Sanchez also uses line repetition, elevating Son/ji's militant rhetoric to poeticized speech. She visually wrenches the language away from standard orthography through unusual punctuation, spelling and vocabulary, frequent inclusion of forward slashes, and inconsistent capitalization. While certainly this move privileges pronunciation of the vernacular (common black speech patterns) as central to an authentic production and performance of this play in terms of articulating with a community-based audience, such use of unorthodox orthography is also both artistic and political in nature. Sanchez privileges adaptive patterns of language and formal innovation—lyrical yet visually and aurally disruptive—as devices to caricature standard English, as, for example, when Son/ji cries: "Yes. u. death. i'm calling yr/name. why not me? Stay away from my family." These orthographic innovations are reinforced by poetic form: "i've given u one son—one warrior for yr/apprenticeship. git stepping death for our tomorrows will be full of life/living/births" (42). One of Sanchez's central purposes in developing these strategies is to interrupt and challenge in direct, tangible ways the character of language as it prescribes acceptability and formulates distribution of power.[26] These strategies in the play demonstrate Sanchez's creativity in terms of militant dramatic technique.

Dirty Hearts is an examination of a broader view of oppression. While the play establishes through allegory a critical militant stance concerning the corrupt nature of American white male power, Sanchez also complicates this notion by embracing a developing interest of the Black Arts movement in the worldwide liberation struggle. Rhetoric and publications of Black Arts movement authors and Black Power movement leaders openly considered international instances of imperialism, racism, and military domination.[27] In *Dirty Hearts* Sanchez illustrates an expanded vision through Shigeko, who is, as a Hiroshima maiden, a figure of multiple oppressions. She is an alien—uneducated, physically disfigured, foreign born, and female—living in the United States. Her presence in the play thus targets, in addition to race and gender, international imperialism as an element of the revolutionist's concern, especially when Shigeko describes (in this partial quote) the atomic bombing of Japan:

> i have been under bleached skies that dropped silver
> i have been open flesh replaced by commemorative crusts. . . .
> i have been fed residual death in a bottle (46)

Shigeko's voice reflects the black militancy's connection with global forms of oppression. In an interview, Sanchez describes Shigeko as an oppressed character "identified through tragedy." She argues that the disempowered in the world need to be named: "They need a name to hold onto, to, in a sense, help them see themselves as identified. They also need a name . . . so that when they are either wiped out or thrown out or kicked out or paternalized, they will be noted" (Wood, 127).

In addition to Shigeko, the characters in *Dirty Hearts* include First Man, Second Man, and The Poet—figures of white privilege and power. Then there is Carl—the only black character—a struggling, ostensibly arrogant "blk/capitalist" (47) who is weakened by his self-pity and by his acceptance of a victimization thrust upon him, symbolized by the white characters' actions in the game of Dirty Hearts. Since the purpose of this card game is to finish with the fewest points, at all costs the player must avoid the queen of spades, which carries most of the damning points. As the characters play, Carl consistently receives the dirty queen and explodes in anger at his own lack of power in face of the domination of the white players. He exclaims, "why me again, today? i received the queen of spades yesterday. i don't deserve it" (47). In terms of powerlessness, Shigeko also recognizes her position, "everything. all has been reduced to its simplest terms for me." She is merely "grateful to be alive" (45-46). The white males minimize the extent of her pain and simply laugh at Carl's protest, for they are ensconced in their own sense of privilege and their capacity to manipulate "the game." At the end of the play, First Man escorts Shigeko back to her subservient place as his wife's maid. While he seems to show an outward concern for her, he actually is more interested in his planned "appointment with a beautiful lady" (51). The white characters thus remain unchanged, impervious to the sufferings of the oppressed that are represented here as existing in multiple dimensions of subjugated culture, gender, and race. Such layered dimensions expose the fallacy of dichotomous representations of cultural and military power, raising the question of distinctions in kinds and levels of oppression. Ultimately, the play begins where it ends, with the white male characters as the dominant, empowered figures of the world entering onstage to start the game again. Sanchez uses ritual drama to reveal through allegorical characters the personal anguish and social conflict inherent in this absurd situation where the characters experience the symbolic as the real.[28] *Dirty Hearts* thus sets the stage for the added complexities in rhetoric, form, and subject matter evident in her next three plays, *Malcolm/Man Don't Live Here No Mo; Uh, Uh; But How Do It Free Us?*, and *I'm Black When I'm Singing, I'm Blue When I Ain't.*

Malcolm/Man Don't Live Here No Mo, Sanchez's first drama written completely in verse, was commissioned for children's theater. The play is simpler than her previous dramatic works are but still does not avoid the political complexities of Malcolm X's life. *Malcolm/Man* focuses on certain key events in X's life—his conversion, marriage, and death. The play protests "wite/amurica" and its oppressive treatment of American blacks:

> i tole u i am wite/amurica & i kill
> even/blk/nigguhs who try to fulfill
> their destiny. wite/amurica am I
> & i will never, never, die. (55–56)

Although intended for children, the work engages militant rhetorical modes—ritual movement, expression in colloquial language, refusal of standard orthography, irony, and call for commitment. In his death throes, the character Malcolm exclaims,

> don't worship my death. i will be gone
> u must move on and on and on. (57)

Significantly, in this play Sanchez introduces for the first time elements that will become signal aspects of her subsequent plays: ritual movement and choral expression. Several young players begin the play in the formation of an X, a symbol both of Malcolm's life and his death. The players then act as a shifting chorus, singing many of their lines and forming and breaking apart the X formation. These approaches to theatrical staging are manifestations of Sanchez's developing vision of form and are more thoroughly actualized in the choruses, dance interpretations, and heavy reliance on music evident in her following two plays. These early experiments in *Malcolm/Man* demonstrate Sanchez's evolving approaches to dramatic structure and her commitment to engaging the community, including children, in working toward revolutionary action.

We can turn to Sanchez's next play, *Uh, Uh; But How Do It Free Us?*, to derive again her central criticisms concerning the militant movement community. The play presents one critical issue that runs through each of her other longer plays—the weakening distracted state that was in part a result of unhealthy behaviors in the black militant community. *Uh, Uh* is a haunting depiction of the undermining effects of drug use, chauvinism, and hedonism on some members of the movement. The play also interrogates experimental roles, abusive behavior, and hypocrisy in the black community. For example, through the characters in Group I—Malik, a black activist; Waleesha, his seven-months-pregnant first wife; and Nefertia, his three-months-pregnant second wife—Sanchez examines how one particular influence of black Muslim thought (polygamy) poses a threat to the community and to the movement. The conflict in Group I occurs when Malik's two wives compete for his attention and approval while he searches out other lovers. The characters are so focused on the dynamics of their increasingly unhealthy personal relationships that they lack any serious commitment to the movement. Polygamy, for Sanchez, is thus a distraction from effective militancy and a threat to communal well-being.

In Group II, Sanchez addresses the power dynamics among men and women. Four black male characters (Brother Man, First Brother, Second Brother, Third Brother) and a white male (White Dude) interact with two whores (Black Sister and White Sister) in a series of violent confrontations. The characters reveal their addictions to drugs and perverse sexual behavior. They claim to be committed to the black community and, at the same time, revel in the unchecked power of their illegal dealings in narcotics, bank robberies, racketeering, and pimping. Sanchez exposes the male characters' negative attitudes toward black women, which undermine the sense of community, especially through the words of Brother Man: "Are you just the typical Black/ woman? Always complaining, never satisfied. Always bitching about something. . . . this no-name whore here. Why she could be your sister. Maybe somebody's momma? Hey, whore, is you somebody's momma?" (71). This Group provides a troubling glimpse of hypocrisy, misogyny, and hedonism.

Brother, Sister, and White Woman compose Group III, raising three issues that complicated relationships in the militant movement: politics, romance, and race-mixing. Brother attempts to maintain two love interests—one with his black girlfriend to solidify his militant reputation, and the other with a wealthy white female to bankroll his activism. Due to his eventual frustration in maintaining these two demanding relationships, while really desiring other women as well, Brother abuses Sister both physically and emotionally. Slapping her repeatedly, he demonstrates his shocking disrespect for black women, not unlike that of the male characters in Part II, "You a Black woman bitch . . . You the same as every Black woman . . . You were born to cry in the night" (94). Through Brother's behavior, Sanchez identifies the dangers inherent in the cruelty, arrogance, selfishness, and promiscuity of some militant black males.

The roles of female characters in Groups I, II, and III are also significant. Through them, Sanchez examines issues and influences in the black community, particularly for black women. In Group I, Malik's two wives lose sight of their original laudable efforts to support the movement as they become embroiled in destructive feelings of jealousy and competition. Malik's manipulation of these women's emotions destroys their sense of worth and dignity, rendering them incapable of focusing on their own growth and well-being. Furthermore, the black and white whore figures in Group II experience victimization through one of the most degrading female occupations, prostitution. The whore figures' oppression occurs in a culture that privileges the position of men, no matter how depraved their exercise of power may be—whether drug peddling, verbal abuse, buying sex, or physical violence. In this Group, there is no great distinction between the oppression of white or black women in terms of patriarchy. However, in Group III Sanchez creates a contrast between the opportunities and realities of black women and white women in terms of personal, economic, and political privilege and power. The young black woman in this group, Sister, is forthright, sincere, and committed to the militant cause and to her man, Brother. She eventually becomes so skilled as a speaker for the movement that Brother begins to resent her success. He has chosen her to be his companion strictly to serve his image and describes her as "My Black woman. The woman I'ma gonna show to the world. My choice for the world to see" (80). But he also has a clandestine relationship with White Woman, who provides him secret financial backing. White Woman ostensibly is comfortable with the political nature of her relationship with Brother, claiming an unselfish love and, as a white liberal committed to the militant movement, generously supporting him financially. Early in the play she exclaims, "you two can't get along on the money you're both making. . . . I told you that a long time ago, it's the money that my father got by underpaying Black people for years. It's rightfully yours. . . . I can share you any time as long as you always turn up here" (81).

White Woman's true motivations are in fact far more complicated. As a female representation of Western culture, White Woman signifies the complicity of white women in Western oppressive dominance. Her professed love relationship with Brother is in fact infused with competition and jealousy. Because Brother refuses steady work and claims that all his efforts must go to movement activism, he has no financial stability and is prone to writing bad checks and depending on his women to support him. As a result, White Woman, through her wealth and seeming generosity, becomes a devastating influence on Brother. Her desire amplifies the power inherent in her secret knowledge of Brother's sexual infidelity. She becomes jealous of his other relationship when Sister becomes pregnant. White Woman "coldly" exclaims in response to his attempts to maneuver outside of her power, "Impregnating women is a criteria for revolution? . . . She's tied to you forever. You can leave [me] anytime you want to. You just need . . . want . . . me for my money" (85). White Woman's urge to control the financial mobility of Brother, now intensified by Sister's pregnancy, evolves into an effort to monopolize his emotional life as well. On the other hand, in discovering Brother's unfaithfulness, Sister becomes depressed, lonely, isolated, and suspicious. Her anguish in turn instills a growing sense of guilt in Brother. For White Woman, the familial love that Brother and Sister may have is more than she can accept, and she demands "almost hysterically" and with a "rasping laugh" that, in a private unconventional ceremony, she and Brother "marry one another to each other" (89–90). In agreeing to this demeaning ceremony where he must follow White Woman's commands and repeat her vows, Brother offers up his last vestige of dignity within the relationship and takes leave of her, now a "tired. Disheveled. Obviously worried" man (91). Facing the outrage of Sister in their final confrontation in the play, Brother ultimately demonstrates his anger and his sense of impotency by verbally and physically abusing Sister. In this scene Sanchez characterizes Brother's culpability in the disintegration of this black family. In effect he has internalized his oppression, rehearsing his longing to be a part of what he sees as desirable but cannot attain—wealth, whiteness, political power, the conquest of white women—while rejecting what he sees as destroying his credibility and personal power—Sister's success as poet and activist.

In the play Sanchez seems intent on also emphasizing that White Woman is complicit in the destruction of this black family. Touting herself as a liberal devoted to the cause, White Woman ultimately insists on satisfying her personal, emotional, and sexual needs through the power of whiteness and wealth. Contrasted with Sister, she is a reflection and indictment of white women's roles in imperialist racist behaviors while at the same time she reveals some of the possible egregious effects of white liberalism delivered on militant communities. This juxtaposition reiterates the fixed dichotomy of American race relations as the black militant woman might see it. Brother's guilt resides then in his sin against family and self, and White Woman encourages his self-doubt in the name of supporting the revolution. Similar to Lula as she interacts with Clay in Amiri Baraka's *Dutchman*, White Woman in many ways contains within the white female body the implications of Western power and wields her sexuality as a channel of domination over Brother in his position as oppressed Other. In this manner, White Woman is inscribed within and reproduces white patriarchal monetary and racial power. Her incitement of Brother's cheating renders his black family nearly paralyzed or, at the very least, causes its division. White Woman is a metonymical affirmation of American racial practice, as her lack of a specific name indicates. Sanchez's examination of the complicity of white women in patriarchal racial domination reveals an interesting developing theme in drama of this period.[29] White racist power personified in white womanhood points to an unfolding division between white and black women in terms of issues of feminism, privilege, and equality during the militant period. Such portrayals in Sanchez's three sequences of *Uh, Uh; But How Do It Free Us?* acknowledge the importance of black women's concerns at a time when they were all but ignored in male-dominated militant discourse and illustrate Sanchez's interest in engendering a distinct black female voice.

Finally, in terms of structure, while centering on the issue of the moral and social deterioration of the militant community, Sanchez incorporates rhetorical strategies into *Uh, Uh* that include shifts in language and form. Her challenges to linearity expand a central element of ritual drama—the refusal of traditional plot line—in creating three

Groups, not ostensibly connected, yet ultimately working toward an accumulation of meaning. She also employs choral dance, music, and iterative symbolic characters.

Sanchez's last produced play to date, *I'm Black When I'm Singing, I'm Blue When I Ain't*, written in 1982, is still compelling and relevant. The play presents Afrocentric visions of history and heritage as central to African American militant experience. A major cultural development in the black community and strongly visible element of black militant discourse of the 1960s and 1970s, Afrocentricity offers an epistemological rubric that privileges black American cultural production—art, literature, social structures, and sciences—as informed by African precepts. The approach is aimed at recuperating and celebrating the focal role of African worldview in the development of African American life, recognizing literary and cultural practices that embrace, rehearse, and reaffirm African traditions. Afrocentricity is directly addressed in the philosophies of militant critics of the period; authors such as Malauna Karenga, Amiri Baraka, and Larry Neal turned to perspectives of African civilizations and the African diaspora.[30] This Afrocentric stance had deep-reaching effects on other militant authors, including Sanchez, as *I'm Black When I'm Singing* illustrates. In the militant Afrocentric perspective, African cultural performatives, in particular art and music, are fundamental positive influences on and outcomes of the black struggle. Reflecting this perspective, triumph of cultural reaffirmation is a central theme of *I'm Black When I'm Singing*. Sanchez also broaches new problems facing the black community—an increasing disillusionment with the polarized notions of the Black Power movement; the seemingly irreconcilable conflict with American material affluence and social education; and the struggle for a black, solvate identity. All are issues that continue to challenge African Americans in the post-militant period.

In the play, the main character, Reena—a gifted young musician and singer—is confined to an insane asylum because of numerous personal traumas in her life. In response to familial rejection primarily because of her dark black skin, she suffers from severe self-loathing. Her mother is both color-struck and judgmental, her husband, abusive and controlling. As a result, Reena suffers from multiple personality disorder. This central conflict of the play is informed by similarities of Reena's selves to four historical black female singers. As Sanchez observes, "The person speaking [Reena] is maybe a Nina Simone type, a strong woman and, sometimes, off kilter for a minute. And there's a Bessie [Smith] type and a Billie Holiday type. And there's the one who is going to replace Nina, a Dianne Reeves kind of person or Abbey Lincoln type, who is much more settled" (Wood, 128).[31] Reena does reflect in some ways the character of the singer/pianist Nina Simone. A classically educated musician who studied at Julliard, Simone performed all over the world.[32] However, the mainstream audience's lack of connection with Simone's original approach to musical form and performance (in blues/jazz piano and vocals) relegated her appeal to a distinct audience; she was more known for her work at clubs, festivals, and concerts than for popularity on American music charts. In addition, her strong personality at times caused conflict with audiences and producers alike. Her celebrity status, as a result, has ultimately been more intense with European audiences (Roland, 105–6). Like Simone, Reena is an accomplished musician but struggles with criticism, in this case from within her own family. Also, like the other selves she manifests in the play, Reena can be seen as a symbolic representation of the times in which the historical models lived. For example, Reena, like Nina, manifests conflicted attitudes and behavior that reflect in some ways the racial upheaval of the 1950s and 1960s in America, exposing the incomplete and shifting social struggle of the period.

Reena's other personalities, also gifted and famous singers, represent different periods in the development of African American music and history. Mama B, hailing from a lower-class background, comes out of the raucous twenties and thirties and ultimately dies because of the blatant inequities in American race culture of that period. She resembles in many ways the blues singer Bessie Smith, who became well known in the early 1920s for her earthy, engaging performances. Sanchez reconstructs, in Mama B, Smith's contempt for middle-class values and behavior. Smith is most often described as a large, often unruly woman whose career began with traveling minstrel groups, performing in small juke joints primarily throughout the South. She eventually became quite successful in vaudeville and in theaters and nightclubs in northern cities with large black populations. A pioneer in blues and soul music, Smith was early on regarded by more traditional black musicians, particularly religious performers, as low, crass, and sinful. However, she was immensely popular with the general black audience. In six months, her first Columbia recording sold over 700,000 copies (Hine, Brown, and Terborg-Penn, 1075). She went on to record with greats like Coleman Hawkins and Louis Armstrong.

Three significant moments in Smith's life are interpreted via Mama B in *I'm Black When I'm Singing*. Bessie Smith did lose an early contract for behaving unprofessionally by spitting during a recording session. Also, she was notorious for excessive eating and drinking and for frequenting a section of Detroit referred to as "buffet flats," which was known for sexual experimentation and homosexuality (1076–78). And as is presented in Mama B's portrayal, Smith died from injuries in a car accident when the nearest hospital would not tend to her because she was black.[33]

Another of Reena's personalities, Toni, a ten-year-old victim of a rape for which she is blamed, ultimately is abandoned to a cruelly institutionalized existence in a rigid Catholic home for wayward girls. Toni's character is closely akin to another famed model singer, Billie Holiday. Holiday attained unprecedented notoriety and praise as a jazz singer from the 1930s through the 1950s. Her life was haunted with tragedy, beginning with a violent rape when she was not yet in her teens, followed by miserable years in a Catholic girls' school and, later, prostitution, until she finally encountered her first singing break. She was imprisoned for drug possession, and she finally died from a heroin overdose at the age of forty-four.[34] Because Toni, like Holiday, experiences similar early traumas, she too seeks solace in the abuse of drugs. In the play, Toni experiences and represents the hedonistic forties. She is finally overcome by fame and drug use, succumbing to mental illness as her final escape.

It is ultimately Malika, Reena's final alter-ego from the Afrocentric seventies, who provides a unifying consciousness that heals all of these personalities. Her most likely real-life model is the jazz singer Abbey Lincoln. Lincoln, who is celebrated for her songwriting, singing, and acting, studied African music and eventually changed her name to Aminata Moseka. She has appeared in films with Ivan Dixon, Gloria Foster, and Sidney Poitier (Hine, Brown, and Terborg-Penn, 721–22). Lincoln's centered nature, her ease with multicultural art and entertainment, and her deep interest in African music and culture have led her to work with some of the most influential jazz ensembles and earned her a reputation as a strong and gifted musical and cultural leader.[35]

I'm Black When I'm Singing culminates in a unification of personality through the healing nature of Lincoln's counterpart, the character Malika. She is Reena's positive, coherent, and racially grounded final identity. Malika proudly expresses her claim to a rich African heri-

tage and to her race's unique contributions to American social and xli
political history. At the end of the play, Malika demonstrates a faith
in black heritage and attempts to convince Reena to allow her to take
over her divided personality: "I will restring these eyes so beauty will
fall from them like diamonds. . . . I will rethread your tongue with
silken words. . . . I will rock you in Blackness so you will grow to love
yourself" (121–22). Through these crafted characterizations, we see a
vision of cultural rootedness as part of Sanchez's solution toward a
healthy black community. Furthermore, Sanchez through these character symbolisms ultimately rejects the strident activist tones of her
earlier plays, while still emphasizing the theme of continued struggle
toward developing strength in community.

Also, the drama privileges an ongoing African American awareness
of postcolonial thought,[36] acknowledging the complexity of self and
communities as they are affected by racial, gendered, and political
oppression. *I'm Black When I'm Singing* thus challenges narrow views
of African American psychological health within the frame of intra/
interracial bigotry and oppression. For example, Sanchez's characters
demonstrate Fanonian theoretical premises concerning the psychological effects of racist oppression as seen in international settings.
Fanon, as well as other race theorists, provides foundational argu-
ments for postcolonial examination of survival, let alone restoration,
of racially besieged self-hoods.[37] Sanchez emphasizes the necessity
of understanding, acquiring, and celebrating cultural education as a
central solution to the rehabilitation and preservation of healthy black
communal identities. As Malika declares at the end of the play, "We've
got to change the sound of our kin / From fear, Silence, Screams in
the nite to / Oooh—oooh—ay—ay—yee—ya—ya. . . . *She does a warrior
dance.* . . . *After the cast comes on, they dance one more sequence and freeze
with their hands in a fist*" (124–25). The play, then, illustrates Sanchez's
affinity with postcolonial theory and strategies.

Sanchez demonstrates through *I'm Black When I'm Singing* a consis-
tency of vision concerning the necessity for psychological vigilance
and cultural activism in the black community, applicable also on a
global scale. This vision is further enhanced by her own continued
political activism into the twenty-first century—her lectures, her in-
volvement in numerous national and international political organi-
zations, her contemporary rhetoric. Thus *I'm Black When I'm Singing*,
while over twenty-five years old, evidences Sanchez's artistic growth
and indicates her awareness of the shifting experiences, needs, and

developments of African American community, a growth of under-standing also progressively evidenced over the years in her numerous volumes of poetry.

Sanchez's most recent play, 2 x 2, provides a personal examination of the impact of activism and generational difference as these have over time variously affected the black community. She reexamines a familiar conflict introduced in her first play, *The Bronx Is Next*—youth-ful activist enthusiasm confronting the fearful paralysis of older gen-erations and of the integrationist mentality of many during the pre-Black Power era. In 2 x 2, Sanchez reminds us that many of the issues that plagued early black communities continue to exist—if in different forms and varying dynamics. Completed in the spring of 2009, 2 x 2 is the most recent opportunity Sanchez offers us to examine through a new play the next stages, as she sees them, in the ongoing legacy of the Black Power movement in the lives of men and women in black America.

Artistic Significance

Through her work as an experimental playwright, Sanchez certainly has added breadth to black militant drama and to the heritage of black women dramatists. Her bold approaches to dramatic structure, lan-guage, and production of meaning were, in fact, contemporary to and consociate with the unique early work of playwrights like Adrienne Kennedy. For example, Sanchez's creation of cumulative "memory visions" and onstage shifts in scene through props and costumes in *Sister Son/ji* parallel in some ways Kennedy's unusual "dream land-scapes" in *Funnyhouse of a Negro* (1964) or *The Owl Answers* (1965). Such elements also anticipate Ntozake Shange's "dream-memories" in her play *boogie woogie landscapes* (1979).

Sanchez's works have also been anticipatory of the innovations of many young successful black women playwrights even into the twenty-first century. Sanchez's artistic efforts foreshadow Shange's and Suzan-Lori Parks's radical reconfigurations of black drama. For example, in creating Groups rather than scenes or acts in *Uh, Uh; But How Do It Free Us?*, Sanchez offers an alternative dramatic structure that creates layered meaning via implication, repetition, synecdoche, and metonymy. These innovations are precedent to Parks's "drama of accumulation" evident in *Imperceptible Mutabilities of the Third Kingdom* (1986), *The Death of the Last Black Man in the Whole Entire World* (1989), or *Topdog, Underdog* (winner of 2002 Pulitzer Prize).[38] Also in *Uh, Uh*, Sanchez incorporates dancers and movement, providing communal and moral commentary on the action within each grouping. Here again she anticipates Shange's use of the specialized dramatic choreopoem, as in *for colored girls who have considered suicide when the rainbow is enuf* (1976).[39]

In *I'm Black When I'm Singing, I'm Blue When I Ain't*, use of choruses also demonstrates Sanchez's continued privileging of choral figures as community voice, anticipating performative audience interaction evident in experimental plays like Robbie McCauley's *Sally's Rape* (1992). *I'm Black When I'm Singing* is also an immensely interesting development in her playwriting and has helped establish the pivotal, organic role that Sanchez has played in first expressing black militant polemics; in establishing a significant female voice as foundation for future black dramatists; in courageously offering a forward-thinking, self-conscious criticism of the movement itself; and in her ultimate shift toward a quest for a global hermeneutics of oppression in its many forms. Sanchez has continued to demonstrate over time her consistent interest in drama. *I'm Black When I'm Singing, I'm Blue When I Ain't* and *2 x 2* have led us from her work in the mid-twentieth century into the twenty-first.

One concern remains in all of Sanchez's work: her unbending commitment to community and to the development of her art. She has thus indelibly impacted the legacy of black drama and politics. Today, Sanchez continues to write and perform her poetry and is currently working on a new play, several volumes of poetry, and a memoir. Her current working draft in drama looks back at the Black Power movement through voices of early activist women of the militant period who have grown old with wisdom and perspective (personal interview, May 5, 2009). She demonstrates here her continued effort to answer with her own voice the deliberate quest for continued African American, and black feminist, consciousness.

This collection assembles all five of the plays that Sanchez has written and published: *The Bronx Is Next, Sister Son/ji, Dirty Hearts, Uh, Uh; But How Do It Free Us?*, and *Malcolm/Man Don't Live Here No Mo*. The collection also includes her unpublished plays *I'm Black When I'm Singing, I'm Blue When I Ain't* and *2 x 2* and two essays by Sanchez—"Ruminations and Reflections," previously published in Mari Evans's *Black Women Writers*, and the preface to *Uh, Uh; But How Do It Free Us?*, previously published in Ed Bullins's *The New Lafayette Theatre Presents*. Also included is "Poetry Run Loose: Breaking the Rules," a new, unpublished essay that Sanchez wrote for this collection. Sanchez's plays have not been archived in print nor placed in library collection. This anthology is thus designed to present the dramatic works of Sonia Sanchez as a source for research and teaching, particularly in terms of revisiting the feminist dramatic voice in black revolutionary art.

Notes

1. This and all further citations of Sanchez's essays and plays refer to this volume.

2. Sanchez's poetry career began in 1966 when her first poems appeared in *Afro-Arts*, a magazine edited by Ysef Iman and published by the Afro-American Arts Festival in Newark, New Jersey. Other early poetry saw publication in LeRoi Jones's and Larry Neal's anthology *Black Fire* in New York in 1968, Dudley Randall's collections *For Malcolm* in 1967 and *Black Poetry* in 1969, and Clarence Major's *New Black Poetry* in 1969.

3. For additional biographical information concerning Sonia Sanchez, see "Sonia Sanchez: The Will and the Spirit" in D. H. Melhelm, *Heroism in the New Black Poetry: Introductions and Interviews* (Lexington: University Press of Kentucky, 1990), 133–79; or Kalamu ya Salaam, "Sonia Sanchez," *Dictionary of Literary Biography Volume 41: Afro-American Poets since 1955*, ed. Trudier Harris and Thadious Davis (Chapel Hill, N.C.: Gale Group, 1985), 295–306.

4. See, for example, Haki Madhubuti, "Sonia Sanchez: The Bringer of Memories"; Houston Baker, "Our Lady: Sonia Sanchez and the Writing of a Black Renaissance" in Gates, ed., *Reading Black, Reading Feminist*; and Franzelle De Lancey, "This Is Not a Small Voice," *B. Ma: The Sonia Sanchez Review* 1 (1995): 30–51.

5. In accordance with popular usage, I use the terms *black* and *African American* interchangeably in this essay. Following the majority of recent critical texts, I also have chosen not to hyphenate the phrase *African American*.

6. There is often a distinct difference in the understanding of community as blacks see it in relation to traditional Western perspectives of community. Most white Americans are "socialized" to think of community collectively but ultimately still in terms of a group of individuals. Yet the sense of community in African American experience is historically and necessarily different as a result of the social effects of slavery and racism, and the often unacknowledged survival of African cultural influences. Community for Africans is the center of human existence. Contrary to many European perspectives, the African worldview values the individual only in relation to others, embracing the correlative "I am

because we are." Black revolutionary artists are in part revolutionary in their call for communal awareness and activism because they alter the individualist image of the artist, and see him/her as, rather, expressing, celebrating, and serving the community.

7. In addition to her literary achievement, Sanchez has demonstrated out-standing commitment as a political activist as well. Her efforts toward justice and equality are evidenced in her early and continued affiliation for over thirty years with the women's organization MADRE, her service as a member of the advisory board for the Women's International League for Peace and Freedom, and her work with PEN, an international writers' organization for justice. She has received the Community Service Award from the National Black Caucus of State Legislators; the Peace and Freedom Award from the Women's International League for Peace and Freedom; recognition as a Ford Freedom Scholar; and the Governor's Award for Excellence in the Humanities. As early as the 1950s, Sanchez became active in the student-run Congress for Racial Equality (CORE). She taught and participated in the black studies movement at San Francisco State College (now University) and developed black studies curricula at several other institutions, including the University of Pittsburgh, Rutgers University, City College of New York, and the University of Pennsylvania. In 1973 Sanchez joined the Nation of Islam in Chicago, working actively with their programs toward black economic and political uplift until 1975. She joined the faculty at Temple University in 1976 and has for over thirty years continued teaching and inspiring her students and impressing critics through her ongoing commitment to global activism, creative writing, lecturing, and teaching.

8. It is important to acknowledge that while Sanchez adamantly challenged the masculinist stance of the male revolutionary dramatists, she did not question their use of homophobic language. In fact, Sanchez herself used such language and images in her own early writing. This blind spot is not one easily reconciled with her obvious concern for equality and for addressing oppression head on. At this early period, much like the male writers, Sanchez still had work to do in terms of recognizing versions of oppression outside of the movement's immediate interests. Yet Sanchez seems to accomplish this fairly quickly. By her third play, *Dirty Hearts*, she begins to express a broader understanding of the breadth of oppression, including in this play the Hiroshima maiden as a new kind of Other. However, it is not until *Does Your House Have Lions?*, her full-length study on the ravages of AIDS, that we see some sympathetic reference, albeit indirect, to homosexuality.

9. Certainly there were black male contemporaries who eventually ex-pressed sensitivity to the issues of black women's quests for equal

recognition. In 1979, Kalamu ya Salaam, in "Women's Rights Are Human Rights!," *Black Scholar* (March–April 1979): 9–14, declared that "any discussion of human rights should include a discussion of women's rights" (9). Later Calvin Hernton would strongly argue the black woman's case in *The Sexual Mountain and Black Women Writers* (New York: Anchor Books, 1987).

10. These women include, among others, the poets Nikki Giovanni, Gwendolyn Brooks, Mari Evans, Johari Amini, Carolyn Rodgers, and the dramatists Lorraine Hansberry, Martie Charles, Alice Childress, Adrienne Kennedy, Barbara Ann Teer, and, later, Ntozake Shange. They are key voices for black feminism and black freedom writing from the 1950s through the 1970s and beyond. In terms of black female dramatists, Lorraine Hansberry's success offered to younger female playwrights an encouraging example as they began to develop their own creative imaginations. Adrienne Kennedy, Sanchez's contemporary in drama, demonstrated a revolutionary vision that was clearly unique. Through the struggles of primarily racially mixed women, her work contradicted the polarized race polemics of many Black Arts movement dramatic theorists and playwrights, often earning her their disdain. Ntozake Shange, who began to write shortly after much of Sanchez's drama was completed, endured significant defamation from black male critics because of her pioneering spirit in directly confronting intra-racial sexism and violence, in, for example, her play *for colored girls who have considered suicide when the rainbow is enuf*. Barbara Ann Teer was perhaps the most visible revolutionary female playwright other than Sanchez. Teer took an innovative approach to drama, developing a company—the National Black Theatre (NBT) or Sun Theatre, which emphasized and celebrated cultural nationalism and ritualized consciousness-raising as fundamental to Black Arts tradition, especially in her productions *Soljourney into Truth* and *Revival*. Sanchez participated in numerous NBT ritual performances, an affirmation of her interest in ritual as a black militant rhetorical strategy. Other important female playwright/directors who actually created their own theater groups throughout the decades of the sixties and seventies include Cynthia Belgrave, Vinette Carroll, and Marjorie Moon. For further information on these and other black female poets and playwrights of the period, see Hill and Hatch, *A History of African American Theatre* (2003); Reid, *Black Protest Poetry* (2001); Steven Carter, *Hansberry's Drama: Commitment and Complexity* (Urbana: University of Illinois Press, 1991); Neal Lester, *Ntozake Shange: A Critical Study of the Plays* (New York: Garland Press, 1995); and Williams, *Black Theatre in the 1960s and 1970s* (1985).

11. See, for example, the agitprop (agitation-propaganda) plays of communist revolutionaries; the absurdist experimental plays of Europe exempli-

fied by the work of Bertolt Brecht or Alfred Jarry; Augusto Boal's Theatre
of the Oppressed; or Ngugi Wa Thiong'o's African Revolutionary Theater
of the Kenyan masses.

12. While Ed Bullins invited Sanchez to publish her first play, *The Bronx is Next*, in his first edition of *New Plays from the Black Theatre*, this drama actually debuted in *The Drama Review*. Sanchez was thus published in TDR's key Black Revolutionary Theatre and Theatre of Black Experience issue of Summer 1968. Contributors to this issue were Ed Bullins, Larry Neal, Ben Caldwell, LeRoi Jones, Marvin X, Ron Milner, and Woodie King. Sanchez was the only female revolutionary playwright included. Bullins did publish Sanchez's second play, *Sister Son/ji*, in his *New Plays from the Black Theatre* anthology. *Uh, Uh; But How Do It Free Us?* was published in another of Bullins's anthologies, *The New Lafayette Theatre Presents*.

13. For information concerning the political unrest of the sixties, consult David Farber, *The Age of Great Dreams: America in the 1960s* (New York: Hill and Wang, 1994) or David Chalmers, *And the Crooked Places Made Straight: The Struggle for Social Change in the 1960s* (Baltimore: Johns Hopkins University Press, 1996).

14. No lengthy, detailed study exists concerning the relationships of black periodicals/black theater critics and militant playwrights and their productions. A definitive sourcebook spanning African American theater history that examines the nature and impact of the relationship between black media/critics and black playwrights is sorely needed.

15. Vol. 12, no. 4 (the 1968 Summer Book) of the *Drama Review* boasted Ed Bullins as invited guest editor. Bullins based his selections on black drama as it portrayed black issues for a black audience, emphasizing an identification of two types, Black Revolutionary Theater and the Theater of Black Experience. The chief editor of the *Drama Review* at the time, Richard Schechner, describes this effort as "the index of a social as well as aesthetic situation" and agreed to allow Bullins editorial freedom (25). Bullins, as a result, selected and organized pieces, creating a special issue that quickly became a manifesto for black revolutionary theater. The issue is still seen as a key text in the establishment of black theater history and aesthetics.

16. These women playwrights must be considered separately from Lorraine Hansberry, Alice Childress, and Adrienne Kennedy, also Sanchez's contemporaries and also furiously concerned with issues of equality, community, and black identity (with the two latter playwrights quite prolific by comparison). These playwrights should be regarded as special cases, however, because they were for the most part not seen as directly connected to the militant movement and were probably more readily produced and reviewed precisely because of this perceived distance. Other

active women playwrights of the militant period such as Barbara Mollette, Barbara Ann Teer, and Sarah Webster Fabio wrote fewer works but were vocal, visible, and recognized in acting, production, criticism, and direction.

17. For information on the Black Codes, see Woodward, *The Strange Career of Jim Crow* (1966).

18. See Charles Lofgren, *The Plessy Case: A Legal-Historical Interpretation* (New York: Oxford University Press, 1987), for a historical description of this case.

19. A specific description of the horrid conditions black children faced in southern public schools is evident in the journals of Charles Houston, the eminent dean of Howard University's law school and special counsel to the NAACP during the 1930s and 1940s. In his fact-finding travels in the South, Houston discovered unequal, deplorable conditions in public schools for blacks. His notes for a trip in 1934 concerning South Carolina's Chester County schools indicate that at Pleasant Grove School "the county furnishes nothing except teachers and two tons of coal per year. Students have to provide their own blackboards, erasers, crayons, stoves, extra fuel, and make most of the repairs on the building." In Richland County, at Moore's Pond School the "nearest drinking water is across the highway at the abandoned gas station. . . . The children sit together on benches. No desks, no chairs, an old piece of blackboard." Ironically, he continues that there is an "abandoned white school about a mile away. Curtains still at the windows. The building is full of desks and other school equipment not in use. The white children are transported 17 miles away into Columbia to school; but the authorities will not permit the Negroes to use either the abandoned building or the abandoned equipment" (quoted in Kluger, 205).

20. For more information, see Charles J. Ogletree Jr., *All Deliberate Speed: Reflections on the First Half Century of* Brown v. Board of Education (New York: W. W. Norton, 2004).

21. For further information on the Black Panther Party, see Hilliard and Weise, *The Huey P. Newton Reader* (2002), and Judson L. Jeffries et al., eds., *The Black Panther Party [Reconsidered]* (Baltimore: Black Classic Press, 1998).

22. See Clayborne Carson, *In Struggle: SNCC and the Black Awakening of the 1960s* (Cambridge, Mass.: Harvard University Press, 1995).

23. Analysis of such an interpretation of African American oppression as political and social colonization is evident in a number of black militant writings, heavily influenced by international political theorists such as Che Guevera, Mao Zedong, and Franz Fanon. Fanon especially examined the effects of domination upon peoples within their own countries. In

his famed text "Lettre au Ministre-Resident" he observes that "the Arab,

permanently alienated in his native land, lives in a state of absolute de-
personalization. The status of Algeria? A systematized de-humanization"
(quoted in Gorden, Sharpley-Whiting, and White, 3). In *The Wretched of the
Earth*, Fanon reiterates such observations concerning the psychological
detriment of colonization on those oppressed: "Because of its systematic
negation of the other person and the furious determination to deny the
other person all attributes of humanity, colonialism forces the people it
dominates to ask themselves the question constantly: 'In reality, who
am I?'" (250). Uncanny similarities between such descriptions and those
of the experiences of the enslaved and subsequently disenfranchised
African American were not lost upon active members in the Black Power
movement. For example, Stokely Carmichael, in 1967, argued that "black
people are legal citizens of the United States with, for the most part, the
same legal rights as other citizens. Yet they stand as colonial subjects
in relation to the white" society. This institutional racism has another
name: colonialism" (*Black Power*, 5, 6).

24. For further study of these and other elements of black rhetoric, see Jackson and Richardson, eds., *Understanding African American Rhetoric: Classical Origins to Contemporary Innovations* (2003).

25. After the bombing of Hiroshima in the Second World War, a number of
maimed women immigrated to the United States. These women, who ac-
quired the moniker "Hiroshima maidens," were severely disfigured and
attempted to begin new lives in a new country. For related information
on Japanese women and the effects of the atomic bomb, see Lequita
Vance-Watkins and Aratani Mariko, eds., *White Flash-Back Rain: Women of
Japan Relive the Bomb* (Minneapolis: Milkweed Editions, 1995).

26. Interestingly, Sanchez's experiments with orthography anticipate a
similar fascination with the political richness of language exhibited in
Ntozake Shange's drama. In a critical discussion of black dramatic language, Shange argues that American Standard English "perpetuates the
notions that cause pain to every black child as he/she learns to speak
of the world & the self" ("Program Note," 21). This stance on language
invites a concerted emphasis of black self-representation in a language
more reflective of black experience. Her response to the "language of
racism" is to succeed in "outdoing the white man in the acrobatic dis-
tortions of english. . . . i cant count the number of times i have viscerally
wanted to attack deform n maim the language that i waz taught to hate
myself in" (21). Not long after Sanchez published her fifth play, *Uh, Uh; But
How Do It Free Us?*, Shange began producing pieces that also employed
unorthodox visual representation of English. Both Sanchez and Shange
theoretically and actively establish, as few other early black female poet/

dramatists have, a self-conscious revolutionary orthography as vehicle for artistic and political resistance.

27. For example, from 1966 through 1975, Digane Joe Goncalves, editor of the first major magazine of poetry in the Black Arts movement—*Journal of Black Poetry*, based in San Francisco—made a point of including African, Asian, Caribbean, and other international radical poetic voices in the journal. Other examples of this broad scope occur in the rhetoric of many black activists. For example, in his description of Black Panther community goals, Huey Newton argues that the Panthers "are . . . individuals deeply concerned with the other people of the world and their desires for revolution" ("Intercommunalism," 185).

28. The word *absurd* is used here in a broadly existential sense. Ritual acts, while seemingly fraught with religious implication, can also be viewed as empty repetitions acted out in search of cohering one's state of being. In the face of the incongruities of racial oppression as unavoidable influences on the lives of the marginal, the repeated efforts of Shigeko or Carl (or even the estranged Poet) to utter through litany their sense of alienation and disempowered isolation seem, in light of the outcome of the play, to indicate for them a perplexing existential discordance that cannot be resolved.

29. Adrienne Kennedy, for example, presents similar kinds of white female figures in several of her plays. Rosemary in *A Rat's Mass*, the Duchess of Hapsburg and Queen Victoria in *Funnyhouse of a Negro*, and the White Dog character in *A Lesson in Dead Language* are all powerful studies of white female complicity with patriarchal racism. All these plays are collected in her anthology *In One Act*.

30. For a general discussion of the role of African heritage in the African American theater, see Hatch, "Some African Influences on the Afro-American Theatre," (1990). For discussion of Afrocentricity in the works of black militant playwrights, see Nigun Anadolu-Okur, *Contemporary African American Theater: Afrocentricity in the Works of Larry Neal, Amiri Baraka, and Charles Fuller* (New York: Garland Press, 1997).

31. A specific study of the relationship of Sanchez's characters to historical musical figures can be found in Karen Turner Ward's unpublished "Creating Four Distinct Characters by Using Historical Models in a Production of Sonia Sanchez's *I'm Black When I'm Singing, I'm Blue When I Ain't*" (Master's thesis, Virginia Commonwealth University, 1985).

32. For more information concerning Nina Simone, see Simone's *I Put a Spell on You: The Autobiography of Nina Simone with Stephen Cleary* (1991; reprint, Cambridge, Mass.: Da Capo Press, 2003).

33. For more information on the life of Bessie Smith, see Chris Albertson, *Bessie* (New Haven, Conn.: Yale University Press, 2003), and Daphne

Duval Harrison, *Black Pearls: Blues Queens of the 1920s* (New Brunswick, N.J.: Rutgers University Press, 1988).

34. More discussion of the life of Billie Holiday can be found in David Margolick, *Strange Fruit: Billie Holiday, Café Society, and an Early Cry for Civil Rights* (Philadelphia: Running Press, 2000), and Donald Clark, *Wishing on the Moon: The Life and Times of Billie Holiday* (New York: Viking Press, 1994).

35. See the *New Grove Dictionary of Jazz*, ed. Barry Kernfield (New York: Grove's Dictionaries, 2002), and Gene Seymour, "Now's the Time for Abbey Lincoln," *Fan Fare* (November 17, 1991).

36. Postcolonial theory examines the history of European imperial powers and their oppression through colonization of other cultures, including those of Africa, India, the Caribbean, and South America. This theoretical approach engages the impact of oppression on language, psychology, self-perception, and cultural practices of colonized societies and individuals within those societies. Because oppression of specific groups within the United States is similar to that of European imperialism, the experiences of groups such as Native Americans and African Americans in the United States can be scrutinized from a postcolonial perspective. See Bill Ashcroft, Gareth Griffiths, and Helen Tiffin, *The Empire Writes Back: Theory and Practice in Post-Colonial Literatures* (London: Routledge, 1989).

37. In particular, Sanchez's play invokes Fanon's Freudian stance that the Negro suffers from a psychopathology steeped in the complexities of colonial oppression. As Fanon argues in *Black Skin, White Masks*, "One should investigate the extent to which the conclusions of Freud or of Adler can be applied to the effort to understand the man of color's view of the world" (141). For Fanon this approach allows that, according to Freud's theory of "psychic trauma," people of color suffer personal anguish that is racially, culturally induced: "When the Negro makes contact with the white world, a certain sensitizing action takes place. If his psychic structure is weak, one observes a collapse of the ego. The black man stops behaving as an *actional* person. The goal of his behavior will be The Other (in the guise of the white man), for The Other alone can give him worth" (154, 155).

38. See Park's article "From Elements of Style," *The America Play and Other Works* (New York: Theatre Communications Group, 1995), 6–18.

39. Shange discusses the importance of movement and dance extensively in her article "A History: *for colored girls who have considered suicide when the rainbow is enuf*" in *See No Evil: Prefaces, Essays and Accounts, 1976–1983* (1984).

I.

Essays

Poetry Run Loose: Breaking the Rules

(2004)

When I am asked why I decided to write a play, I must say that it is because I actually saw the affinity between being a poet and being a playwright. Every playwright that I liked also wrote poetry. I saw the connection of how closely we pay attention to words as poets. That same kind of attention is paid to the dialogues that we write in plays. So I saw a really kindred kind of spirit going from poetry to the play. I found out once when I was writing a poem that it wasn't going well because so many voices were surfacing. I realized these words, these ideas, these voices really worked better in a play. I moved some of the dialogue that I had been writing into *The Bronx Is Next*, and I realized that indeed this was going to work. That play was part of a trilogy that I had planned. *The Bronx Is Next* was the first play in this trilogy where Blacks were leaving Harlem to return home to the South. The other two plays (not written) were about their trek south and their final settlement. What I found sometimes with poetry is that I was constricted for the first time in my life by the poem. How I moved out of that constriction was through the play. There, what I considered poetry ran loose, as they say. I was able to move the language and use many different words, not just one person's voice as sometimes in a poem, but in different people's voices in a play. And I heard the same kind of majesty that is in the poem in the play.

The challenge for me with drama was realizing that I was going to have to put engaging words in each person's mouth, words that would make for movement on stage. As a consequence, I could not always be introspective; I mean I had to really look up and see how the play, for me was going to end, whereas with the poem that is not the case. Within my head, with my notes that I make in the margins as I'm writing, I always move ahead saying this is going to happen, that's going to happen, this is going to happen. I come back and begin to write the things that I said are going to happen in the play. In writing *The Bronx Is Next*, with the characters, I wanted to have them just be representative, so I have an Old Sister because it is unimportant what her name is. I have a Black Bitch, it's unimportant what her name is, and I have a White Cop. Then I give the others names. They are the key players, the revolutionaries. I start with the scene that's a block in Harlem. We have Charles begin, "Keep 'em moving Roland. C'mon you mothafuckers. Keep moving. Git you slow asses out of here. We ain't got all night. Into the streets. Oh shit. Look old sister. None of that. You can't take those things" (25).

Dr. Arthur Davis, a lovely, wonderful, brilliant professor at Howard University, said that *The Bronx Is Next* is one of the best, well-written plays that he's taught. The question he said to me that always came up for some of the students is did I take the Old Sister back into the house and leave her there? I did. Sending the woman back in there to die is symbolically the killing of the past in order for one to have a future. And the young men do it gently. They do it by giving her something to go to sleep because they know she cannot make the trek. It's not necessarily that there is no respect right here for the old woman, but it's similar to something Harriet Tubman did. Harriet Tubman carried a gun, and when you got on her Freedom Train she said the only way you get off this Freedom Train, if you can't make it, is you die. It was with that idea in mind that one saw the young men moving towards that old woman in that fashion. Just saying we'll put you to sleep old woman; you'll never make this long trek anyway. You'll keep us from making it. So it was to talk about the ideas of some of these young men who had just a very straight point of view of revolution, who could not veer to the left or the right. For them, if someone is there, someone elderly, then they don't make a wheelchair for them to travel in; they will not be detoured.

One does see, however, with the woman called Black Bitch, the conflict between black men and black women at that time. How she had decided to live, how she had decided to make it in the world, how she had decided to move. The men are very angry with her, as they are Black Nationalists. Their Black Nationalist point of view is how dare this woman be making out with this White Cop. And so they treat her in this kind of very negative way, this very cruel fashion. She says at some point, "I only explain the important things. He comes once a week. He fucks me. He puts his grayish white dick in me and dreams his dreams. They ain't 'bout me. Explain him to my boys? Man. I am surviving. This dude has been coming regularly for two years—he stays one evening, leaves and then drives on out to Long Island" (32). She has a really interesting sense of reality. So I have the men throwing up all these ideas that were running rampant at the time. One was concerning the black matriarch, the kind of idea that Moynihan had put into the black community that people adopted without thinking about. The interplay is between the Black Bitch and this so-called strong black man. After he hits her, she gets up and says, "Take your choice—your pick—slap me or fuck me—anyway you get the same charge" (33). It is significant that one young man does stand and say "let me help you." Black Bitch is still going to make the trek with them. And then a very surreal thing happens with the White Cop. The male characters all reverse roles where the White Cop becomes a Black man and the Black men become White Cops, and the White Cop experiences the oppression that occurs to Black men in their community.

When I was up for tenure, there was a committee for my plays, a committee for my poetry, and a committee for my prose. The man who headed the committee for my plays was walking down the hallway one day as I was going to get my mail. He said, "Sonia we are reading your plays; they are really quite good, but who in the world would ever be running down the street and be picked up by a cop"? Was he kidding? It was so weird. The next day I brought my *Times* in to read before class, and right in the *Times* was an article about a young man, at night, running down 125th Street, feeling free, facing the wind, and the cops stopped him and pushed him up against a wall and beat him. So I cut it out and put it in the professor's mailbox, so he could understand that this was not a farfetched kind of thing. To me the most interesting writing was the role-playing that occurred in *The Bronx Is Next*.

When I wrote the play at that time, I show a kind of complexity in the dynamics that are occurring in a black neighborhood, even when there is a revolutionary movement going on. There are the young men who see only one direction to go in. There is a lack of patience for anything that is going to interfere with that move out of Harlem. Within the black neighborhood there are the old, and then there are the young. What this play really questions is that even if you are in a revolutionary movement, you've got to be sympathetic towards the people who live there. You can go in and live a year and find out what they need and then come with your idea of what they need, but you must get to understand them and also to love them. I think that sometimes when people are very young, as these young revolutionaries were, they don't always see the human being; they see always the ideology. However, I wrote that play the way I did because a complexity is established. I end up by saying it's very obvious that if they had really been anti-woman, they would have killed the Black Bitch, but they didn't. In the midst of their ideas about something, they still have to see the reality of folks. The reality is that the Black Bitch had to take care of her children; she did the best that she could. The reality of that Old Sister is that she wanted to take all her things on that road. That was not possible, so they let her then stay with all of her things. She went to sleep with her things, because without those things she would not survive.

While writing *Sister Son/ji*, my second play, I was living in San Francisco and teaching at San Francisco State. Ed Bullins knew I wrote plays, and he asked me if I had a play for this anthology that he was editing. He was editing a collection, *Plays from the New Black Theatre*. I thought the very important thing in a university setting would be to write about a professional woman who had traveled the road that this woman had traveled. I think what is important was for people to see this woman who had aged, who is in the "Age and now and never again" time, to show her movement and evolution. That's why I began with the old. I'm always fascinated with the old and showing how people get to that stage. So this woman is on stage when the curtain goes up, and she's sitting in a rocking chair. She's talking to the audience. I did it poetically. She's talking to people about her life. "i shall be a remembered Sister Son/ji. today i shall be what i was/shd have been and never can be again. today i shall bring back yesterday as it can never be today. as it shd be tomorrow" (37). In this one-act play, this one-woman show, there is this sparse set, just a place for the change of clothing, just the table full of some make-up, and the chair. Therefore, this woman can engage her audience and take them with her wherever she wants them to go. That was the joy of it.

So we begin a logical thing. This play is about a lot of women who were involved with change and revolution and the movement. Coming to it with open arms, willing to struggle for change, willing to teach, willing to have children, willing to struggle and travel and pick up and go all out under the guise that change will happen in this country. This is almost a love song to the women who have done this. A love song to women who realized that they were going to take a chance to do things quite the same as, and differently from, their parents, from their own mothers, and their own grandmothers. They were going to go out into the world and challenge the world. So I present Sister Son/ji next as a young woman in college and the first time she makes love, believing as if that were the key, but finally realizing oh, ok that's what that's about. Well, I've gotten that over with. I can go out into the world in a different way, with a new scent. She says, "nesbitt, do u think after a first love each succeeding love is a repetition?" (39). Certainly she recognizes the fact that this might be the first, but it's not the last.

In a sense, this event predicts what's going to happen to her as she goes out into the world. We hear this young woman learning some of the information that was being disseminated at that particular time. We hear of the Black Power conferences where people are talking over what people should be about and what they should do and how they should straighten out their lives. She internalized that if they didn't straighten out their lives, they would not be able to succeed and survive. They had to get rid of the weed, the alcohol, the drugs, and the womanizing, all the things that kept them from moving in the way that they needed to move. We see the women at some point being involved with revolutionary activities. Some women went crazy involved with the movement, but just as some women go crazy in their homes in the suburbs, just as some women go crazy if they live in the urban city, just as some women go crazy if they live in the Midwest, or some women have gone crazy who live in the South. I show Sister Son/ji going crazy from her immersion in a movement that cannot catch her when she falls down in midnight solitude. And all of a sudden she's singing, "THE HONKIES ARE COMING TO TOWN TODAY. HOORAY. HOORAY. HOORAY. / THE CRACKERS ARE COMING TO TOWN TODAY. TODAY. TODAY. HOORAY" (40). This was intentional. Using terminology that had been learned, and then throwing it back on the self. Recognizing that if she is indeed singing, going crazy, even the terminology perhaps is crazy. The craziness seeps into her bloodstream as she dances her dance of madness.

But name-calling was not what this was all about. This woman's really going crazy during the midnight hours and having to pull herself up and survive, and probably survive by herself. She must deal with everything that is happening in terms of the war and how she loses a couple of her children to the war. At the end of that war, Sister Son/ji says, "Death is a five o'clock door forever changing time. And wars end. Sometimes too late. i am here. still in mississippi. Near the graves of my past." Then she says, "i want to do what all old/dying people do. Nothing. but i have my memories" (43). Ultimately, she challenges the audience, "we dared to pick up the day and shake its tail until it became evening. a time for us. blk/ness. blk/people. Anybody can grab the day and make it stop. can u my friends? or maybe it's better if I ask: WILL YOU?" (43). I have seen many young actors do this piece. Gloria Foster in all her glory performed this role and got great reviews.

One of the places I was going with my next play, *Dirty Hearts*, was to expand the question of oppression. The character Shigeko was a person I actually met. She was one of the Hiroshima maidens who came to the U.S. She was a woman who wore a hat, with a veil to cover her face. We were meeting someplace with an all-women's group. And she took off her hat and revealed her scarred face, and I had to keep looking into her eyes to keep from turning away. Finally, when I talked to her, her very gentle voice made me forget what I was seeing, and I saw behind the scars and burns. I wanted in this play to show the interaction of what is happening with America and the world. The kind of oppression that still continues. It's an oppression that often happens against black folks; it's an oppression that often happens against many others like this young woman who has been scarred for life from the atomic bomb.

When I write, it's in terms of what goes on, not only in my life and with people around me, but I also write in terms of things that I'm doing and also the ever-expanding ideas I have about the world. One of the great things I've always said is that I taught school and also read my poetry to audiences, and, contrary to what people said about us, we always had an audience that was of many races. There were whites, and Asians, Native Americans, and Puerto Ricans sitting down front, listening to what we were saying about this country, and that was the joy. So I knew I always had this multiracial audience engaging me in a conversation.

When I taught in the university, I always had students, the same kind of multiracial students, coming toward me, asking me questions. So there was then the intersection of what is written and what is lived. Many of our early poems and the early plays were things that we did quite often coming from the discovery that we had been enslaved. Also the discovery of people who had moved in such a way as to change things on this earth. Our discovery of Malcolm, our discovery of Martin, our discovery of Frederick Douglass, our discovery of that kind of history/herstory. Our discovery of Africa, our discovery of people in Latin America, our discovery of Neruda. Our discovery of Guillén, our discovery of Chinua Achebe and Ngugi Wa Thiong'o. Our discovery of these people who also challenged the world. We saw them and smiled and knew that we were on the right road.

I have always read. I've understood many of the things that people have been saying about change. I read O'Casey, Yeats, Lorca, and Hughes. I read the 1930s playwrights and the Harlem Renaissance playwrights. As I wrote plays, I read Brecht and learned from him. There are all these connections that were going on for me and for others at the same time. I read other poets. Paul Blackburn was one of my favorite poets. Blackburn was a very gentle man and a very lyrical, very important poet. And he was a friend. I read Baraka's plays and poems and saw his genius, and I and others followed in his gargantuan footsteps, awed by his brilliance and vision. I read Ed Bullins and discerned sites and places and forces that were crucial to our understanding of the Black world. I think simply that there were already the intersections that many of us made on our own, getting to know people, getting to know how they wrote, how they write. We read with all kinds of people. We went on stage, especially the anti–Vietnam War events. This was constant movement that many of us had, going from the first realization that our ancestors had been enslaved in this country. Then the realization of just how discriminated against we were, to be involved in a country that we realized just didn't like us, would never like us, or appreciate us, or the contributions of our ancestors. But at the same time we recognized and realized that it was necessary to move the African American, this African, back on the human stage because he/she had been taken off that stage. That was always the hard thing to do. And certainly it has been important for me, as a consequence, to talk about what it means to be human in the twenty-first century.

So the characters meet to play Dirty Hearts. Dirty Hearts is a card game. I learned how to play when I hit Hunter College at sixteen. Some of the students asked, did I smoke and did I have any cigarettes? I said I didn't have any, but I would go buy some. When I went up to the counter, I was so nervous. They were watching me, this sixteen-year-old with all this long hair down her back looking like a little tiny kid. I was so nervous, I couldn't think of a cigarette to get. So I said, "Camels." There was an ad there with Camels. I brought the Camels back to the table and tried to push them out, and I finally knocked one out. I asked them did they want some, and they all said no. And they proceeded to watch me try to smoke a Camel. I coughed all the way through, and they fell out laughing. The second question was did I know how to play Dirty Hearts? I said no. So they said we'll teach you. Well, they taught me as much as they wanted me to know about the game. They said the purpose of the game was not to get any hearts. That game was much more complex than that, as you see as the play develops. They said you don't want the queen of spades because you get thirteen points for that. But the other strategy is that if someone gets all the hearts and the queen of spades, then everybody else gets twenty-six points. So I wanted to talk about *Dirty Hearts* as that kind of game. Because the point is that Shigeko was there, Carl was there—the Black man, the poet, and the businessmen were there. They all sit down to play this Dirty Hearts game of life. Sometimes you're not given all the information in this place called America, just like the game of Dirty Hearts.

Malcolm/Man Don't Leave Here No Mo I wrote in Pittsburgh for The Liberation School. The children treated it seriously. It was a joy to see them act their parts. I love the use of the chorus in this play. The use of a chorus for me not only reiterates, but also sometimes is very seditious, not in this play necessarily, but in my other plays. Sometimes they're not controllable. The chorus can go off on you. I like this device because, although the chorus is assigned sometimes to make for continuity of a play or to explain and/or to sum up what is going on, its use can also be varied. In *Uh, Uh; But How Do It Free Us?*, for example, without any doubt the chorus is saying to the people up there on the stage, you're full of shit. How in the world are we going to respond to this behavior? The chorus responds in this very real fashion. That's what I mean about being seditious. The chorus sometimes is seditious without even saying a word. It could be a dance chorus, as it is in *Uh, Uh; But How Do It Free Us?* I saw the play done once where the dancing was amazing. They summed it up in a dance. This cocky man walking across the stage with these two women behind him. This is why I took time to show the dance movement in words and in what they did. I just found that at that time I was playing a great deal with dance, and the acting, and the chorus. You can make the chorus be the dancer, the speaker without the words. When I did the chorus in *Malcolm/Man Don't Live Here No Mo*, it was a celebration of Malcolm. The chorus in X formation made for the interplay of the children there. They were making that mark by participating, and making that mark left a mark on them. Those children loved that play. It was the only play I'd written for children, other than *A Trip to Backwards Farm*, which was never published. It too is a little play in poetry that I did for children.

A chorus also is central to *I'm Black When I'm Singing, I'm Blue When I Ain't*, responding to the main character's insanity. I think that if you are so oppressed by the dominant society, as so many people of color have been and are, then the question of insanity is not really if, but rather how much you are. It's a given that there will be some kind of craziness involved. So the whole point of this play is the title, *I'm Black When I'm Singing, I'm Blue When I Ain't*. When I'm blue there is some kind of depression involved. But when I'm on stage, when I'm trying to sing this song that I am singing, I am healthy and quite alive. And I begin the play in perhaps a sanitarium, an insane asylum, or a hospital. The main character, Reena, is humming, and she gives this cryptic observation, "The color of death is grey and white / The color of my life is white and grey / They are different and yet the same" (100). After these first very strict few lines, she continues, "Don't ya know—I learned all of this in a cabaret?" She says again, "The color of this room is white and grey / The color of my mind is grey and white / They are different and yet the same" (100). She goes from life to mind. She goes from room to white and grey; an inversion is there. Next she says, "Don't ya know—A dog licks the hand it's gonna bite?" (100). She's insanely insane. She laughs, she grunts, and then she begins to eat her feces. And the audience is shocked. She responds, "Want some? . . . It ain't too bad. It's solid you know. Don't look so shocked, we eats what we can when we can in this hellhole" (100). Then she remembers her manners. She says something like Hey, Hey. Hold it. I haven't forgot my manners. She offers again. And continues, "Don't look so disgusted. You there sitting in yo' middle-class conformity. You think I'm mad don't you. You should be grateful that I'm offering you this little shit. It's controlled shit. Institutionalized shit. There's so much more of it out there that's running loose. And you always falling in it and always taking it too!" (100). Then she begins this whole discussion about what goes on in the world. What I like about this play is that playfulness and seriousness shift between reality and insanity. It's the kind of beginning I wanted to have, to come to this arena of madness which is sanity, coming to this arena of sanity which is madness.

When I am asked how I see drama as a part of all of my works, it's very difficult to sometimes characterize what I do. Every time I write a play I want to see it performed. But staging a play is a marathon. It has to do with cost, people, venues. That was why it was a joy to see my plays done at the university level. I am currently trying to finish up a play. I've been finishing this play actually for the last two or three years now. I keep going back to it. The reason why I'm not necessarily running towards it is because I'm not sure it will get produced or someone will do it, unless I get it done myself. For this reason, I tend not to rush towards a conclusion. I might rush to a conclusion of a children's book or a book of poetry, or a book of prose. But a play sometimes is not the same. The reason why I finished some of the other plays was because I was asked to do them. I was asked quite frankly can you do a play? Jomandi Productions in Atlanta asked me can you give us a play? And I gave them *I'm Black When I'm Singing, I'm Blue When I Ain't*. At the time, the company was going through a hard time, and I said here's this play. I gave it to them and said you can do with it what you want. They made some money that kept the theater together. Tom Jones and Marsha Jackson were former students of mine at Amherst and Smith. That's why I was so very close to them, and that's why I always tried to give them what they wanted or needed. That was important to continue the tradition.

My playwriting is also important to me because I love it as a craft. I love seeing it on stage. I can see with my eye what works and what doesn't work as I watch it. I remember seeing *I'm Black When I'm Singing, I'm Blue When I Ain't* in production in Atlanta, and after they had done it for me the first time, I said, well, this isn't working. I sat there and told them why it wasn't working. That's how I see it; I see that play, and I see the people moving with my dramatist's eye because I'm involved with that play as a playwright. But, also, I'm involved with the play as a viewer, as an audience too. So I hear and see what's working and what's not working. It's almost like directing. I have always wanted to direct, but I've just never had the time to do that. So when I see a play and it's in production, in a way I can direct it when they ask me, as the author, "Sonia, what do you think?" That's how my direction evolves. When I gave the play to Jomandi, I thought it was important for them to survive. But also it was important to me too, for me to see something I had written, see it being staged, see it developed, and hear the music. I wrote the lyrics for the music, indicating that it was a blues here and it was jazz there. When I heard the musicians, I saw that they had created something that was very important to the play, an intrinsic part of the play actually.

I think when people write, they want someone to read their work. And then certainly someone to comment on it, and certainly someone to hold a dialogue. I love the dialogue that I experience with people when I write. Writing both poetry and drama employs craft. I think that because a poem is perhaps fourteen lines or twenty lines or thirty lines does not mean it has not required much craft. But I think that what happens with the plays is that you use more words. And each line is not necessarily loaded. Each line in a poem I think is loaded. The poet doesn't ever intend to lose the reader. In a play you can almost say some lines are directions or lines can perhaps make the reader or audience hesitate or stop and go someplace else. But the plot, the denouement, the movement at the end, the death that occurs on the stage, the laughter that occurs, the insanity that occurs, the joy that occurs, you have written words that bring an audience to respond. You've painted that picture on that stage, and the audience will cry as they hear those words being spoken, or will laugh, or will see themselves on that stage. The playwright brings people to a point of movement, of ideas, and can bring people to action. They'll think and say I'm glad I'm not that person, but I'm glad I'm here seeing that person.

I studied with Louise Bogan, who taught us that a poet must read his or her poetry well. So I practiced. In reading my poetry on stage, I learned how to bring an audience to tears, or laughter, or stillness. The difference with a play is that maybe three or more other people will do that also, bring an audience to a moment of reflection. I think what *I'm Black When I'm Singing, I'm Blue When I Ain't* did in telling the story of three different women who were in the music business was to talk about the exploitation of these women—be it husband, be it manager, be it audience. With Mama B, the Bessie character, it was the audience's exploitation of her. Audiences would say I love you, I love you. Then she goes to a Buffet Flat. When she's drunk and falls out on the floor, they exploit her. They do not pick her up and say, my dear sister let us take you someplace and let you rest because you have given us so much to stay alive, you've given us so much beauty. They let her wallow in her humiliation. At some point, to me, there always is this ambivalent feeling that an audience has for an artist. It is a feeling always of ambivalence that says simply, I'm not too sure I like what you bring to me half the time. You make me stop, you make me think, you make me feel sorry, you make me angry. It's the artist as suspect, you see.

Some of my plays were done in critique of the movement, as in *Uh, Uh; But How Do It Free Us?* It was a critique that said, don't come to me with this, because I'm going to say, if it don't free us, then I don't want to hear the shit. *Sister Son/ji* was very much a monologue, a woman-for-all-seasons play. This woman literally has to go through the fire. She goes through the fire, and she comes out alive. And she says really at the end, I made it through. Can you go through the fire that is America, and make it through? Here I am, she says. I'm this old woman; I came through. I have survived. Some of my children didn't survive, but I survived. This means that the ideas survived. This lesson of survival began in the first play, *The Bronx Is Next*, and continued to *I'm Black When I'm Singing, I'm Blue When I Ain't*, and continues today.

Ruminations/Reflections

(1984)

. . . *I see myself helping to bring forth the truth about the world. I cannot tell the truth about anything unless I confess to being a student, growing and learning something new every day. The more I learn, the clearer my view of the world becomes. To gain that clarity . . . I had to wash my ego in the needs/ aspiration of my people.*

The poet is a creator of social values. The poet, then, even though he/she speaks plainly, is a manipulator of symbols and language images which have been planted by experience in the collective subconscious of a people. Through this manipulation, he/she creates new or intensified meaning and experience, whether to the benefit or the detriment of his/her audience. Thus poetry is a *subconscious conversation*, it is as much the work of those who understand it as those who make it.

The power that the poet has to create, preserve, or destroy social values depends greatly on the quality of his/her social visibility and the functionary opportunity available to poetry to impact lives.

Like the priest and the prophet, with whom he/she was often *synonymous*, the poet in some societies has had infinite powers to interpret life; in others his/her voice has been drowned out by the winds of mundane pursuits.

Art, no matter what its intention, reacts to or reflects the culture it springs from. But from the very beginning two types of poetry developed. One can be called the *poetry of ethos* because it was meant to convey personal experience, feelings of love, despair, joy, frustration arising from a very private encounter; the other, *functionary poetry*, dealt with themes in the social domain, religion, God, country, social institutions, war, marriage, and death in the distinct context of that society's perception.

To answer the question of how I write, we must look also to why I write. I write to tell the truth about the Black condition as I see it. Therefore I write to offer a Black woman's view of the world. How I tell the truth is a part of the truth itself. I've always believed that the truth concealed or clouded is a partial lie. So when I decide to tell the truth about an event/happening, it must be clear and understandable for those who need to understand the lie/lies being told. What I learned in deciding "how" to write was simply that most folks tend to think that you're lying or jiving them if you have to spice things up just to get a point across. I decided along with a number of other Black poets to tell the truth in poetry by using the language, dialect, idioms, of the folks we believed our audience to be.

The most fundamental truth to be told in any art form, as far as Blacks are concerned, is that America is killing us. But we continue to live and love and struggle and win. I draw on any experience or image to clarify and magnify this truth for those who must ultimately be about changing the world; not for critics or librarians.

Poetry's oldest formal ties were with religion. Humanity's first civilizations, it must be remembered, were theocratic and therefore religiously inspired. Thus were the ancient Black civilizations of the Nile, Mesopotamia, the Indus River, and Meso-America, societies in which religion as a *social vector*, not as *ritual*, exerted a prime force that motivated human action consciously and unconsciously.

Biblical scholars were poets. Marx was a poet. Mao was a poet. The Quran is poetically written. Black people lack such a centralized value network or system of thought. But this allows the poets of each age to contribute to the values of that age. I still believe that the age for which we write is the age evolving out of the dregs of the twentieth century into a more humane age. Therefore I recognize that my writing must serve a dual purpose. It must be a clarion call to the values of change while it also speaks to the beauty of a non-exploitative age.

It is within this dual purpose that many of us see the Black aesthetic. For example, I chant in many of my poems. That chanting calls up the history of Black chanters and simultaneously has the historical effect of old chants; it inspires *action* and *harmony*. In one of my plays, *Sister Son/ji*, Son/ji is at a point of desperation or insanity or pretty close to it—which means that she is crying out in the night and no one listens or hears. She can sit in a rocking chair and sing a spiritual or she can chant the way Sister Son/ji does when she knows she is almost gone or she is close to insanity. As she moves toward the deep end, she chants something that is ancient and religious. She chants her prayer. Her life. Her present. Her past. Her future. And a breath force comes back into her and with this chanting and on her knees she is reborn.

In *Sister Son/ji* and *A Blues Book for Blue Black Magical Women*, I play with the concept of time. If I can give you a Black woman who is old, then is young, mature, and then old again, then I've dealt with time on some level. Then she becomes timeless. And we become timeless. Universal. When we understand the past and present in order to see our future. Therefore to see Son/ji evolve into this old woman still full of hope, with no bitterness in terms of the children and the husband she has lost to war (time), with an understanding that if she can say to the audience *we dared to pick up the day* (time) and *make it night* (time); then to say can you or will you is a cry, a challenge to the audience to be timeless. And you will be timeless if you *be* about constant work and change. Black people will have no beginning or end if each generation does the job it must do to change the world.

Or in some poems I glorify the work or struggle of a sister struggler. Our poetic history needs to grow in this area, just as our consciousness needs to understand how to appreciate women as beautiful human beings.

In *A Blues Book for Blue Black Magical Women*, I attempt to show a Black woman moving/loving/living in America and the consequences of that movement. A "mountaintop" poem. George Kent says that *Blues Book* "possesses an extraordinary culmination of spiritual and poetic powers. It is in part an exhortation to move the rhythms of black life to a high peak through deep and deeper self-possession; in part, a spiritual autobiography." Kent said things that made me rethink/remember what I was doing at that time. I told D. H. Melham in an interview, "Yes. It's true. I was constantly climbing a mountain to get to that poem. And when I got there, two things could have happened. I could have said, 'Goody-goody-goody. I'm here. Look at the rest of you, you aren't.' However, after I was there, I looked up and saw another mountaintop, and then you realize what it's really all about on many levels."

But whatever the area or the issue, I see myself helping to bring forth the truth about the world. I cannot tell the truth about anything unless I confess to being a student, growing and learning something new every day. The more I learn, the clearer my view of the world becomes. To gain that clarity, my first lesson was that one's ego always compromised how something was viewed. I had to wash my ego in the needs/aspiration of my people. Selflessness is key for conveying the need to end greed and oppression. I try to achieve this state as I write.

Writing today in such a complex industrial age, with so many contradictions and confusions, is difficult. Many of us learned that to continue to write, we could not tell the truth and live a lie at the same time. So the values in my work reflect the values I live by and work for.

I keep writing because I realize that until Black people's social reality is free of oppression and exploitation, I will not be free to write as one who's not oppressed or exploited. That is the goal. That is the struggle and the dream.

To bring my thoughts on how and why I write on down to elemental terms, the real nuts and bolts, I'll tell you how all of this gets done.

I must work a full-time job. Take care of a house and a family. Referee or umpire at Little League games. Travel. Carry books when I travel. Work some more. Deal with illnesses and injuries. Help build the political organs within the Black community. Work on the car. Run for trains and planes. Find or create breaks. Then, late at night, just before the routine begins again, I write. I write and I smile as the words come drifting back like some reverent lover. I write columns for newspapers, poems, plays, and stories in those few choice hours before I sleep.

And they say leisure is the basis of culture.

Preface to
Uh, Uh; But How Do It Free Us?
(1972)

From a Conversation
with Ed Bullins, Fall 1972

The reason that I decided to become a playwright is about the same reason I decided to become a poet. That is, one day I sat down and decided to write a play. I write plays, I guess, because I can't say what I want to say in a poem. I have to stretch it out into a play. And a play is a special kind of writing in that it has a lot of dialogue in it. And the dialogue tries to convey messages to people as to what is. *The Bronx Is Next* is the first play that I did. Then I wrote a play called *Dirty Hearts*. Then a play called *Sister Son/ji*, then *Malcolm/Man Don't Live Here No Mo*. And then *Uh, Uh; But How Do It Free Us?* And I'd say they're all similar plays; however, they're all different plays in that the two most important words in "playwright" is write plays. Meaning that you try to show what is right and what is to be played right.

I'm trying to say that when I did *The Bronx Is Next*, I was talking about Harlem and the tenements in Harlem. How people live in Harlem. It was my opinion at the time and it still is that those same tenements need to be burned down. As a consequence in the play I have, I guess, what you'd probably call the militants in the terminology of America. I have some men who decided to move Black people out of Harlem and burn down the tenements.

The Bronx Is Next was the first part of what I call a trilogy where you would have the second part of the play be people making a trip either South or to the Midwest. In between there I haven't done it except for parts in my mind.

At the time I knew that a lot of Black people were dying in the cities. I watched us die. I watched some of us make it as such, meaning that some of us survived. But the majority of Black children, Black young people were dying, being killed in the city called New York. And at the time that I did *The Bronx Is Next*, I thought that one way we could eliminate this dying was for us to leave the city. I knew all of us would not.

You see, some of us need to get back to the land. You know, from whence we came. Some of us need to touch earth, you know, and get—

because we've all come from earth—we need to return to earth which really nourished us. Because the city, the tenements, the stone-cold brick buildings, where we are stuffed on top of each other like mice, are destructive. When you walk down Seventh Avenue and Lenox Avenue and Eighth Avenue in New York City we can say this is all beautiful, this is us, but this devil in this country has made us become almost animals and then he's packed us in buildings like animals. And when I did *The Bronx Is Next*, it was on that level, like we've got to leave.

Now in the play, if you remember, not everyone wanted to leave. But it seems to me at some point in order to like move away from this madness, some of us will have to leave the big cities like New York City just to live and become in a sense human beings. Because living the way we live tends to make us inhumane, tends to make us animals.

I'm not saying that I agree with that premise now, at this time. But at the time that I wrote the play that was the point of making it a "trilogy," and starting out the trek.

I wasn't going to call it the trek, but the movement South or the movement to the Midwest. I thought that would involve the kind of trials and tribulations which in my mind might be unraveled along the way. There were problems among the leaders, the people that led them. There are all kinds of this kind of interplay. It was going to be a longer play than *The Bronx Is Next*.

Each succeeding play was going to be longer than the previous. And then eventually the people would settle someplace, wherever they settled with all those problems that they were going to have. I felt these things very strongly because I was raised in a tenement in New York City. So one understands exactly what happens. The constant dealing with roaches in dingy apartments and too small places and a room that faces a wall. I suppose that's why I wrote a lot. Because if you have a bedroom with the only window in the bedroom facing a wall outside, your imagination is always running rampant. You've got to do something behind that wall.

Because once you stuck your head out the window, garbage hit you in the head coming from the windows above yours. So I guess at the time I wrote because I had ideas, if not ideology; I had ideas or opinions about things being Black in this country. So *The Bronx Is Next* was one of them.

No Black woman even like nowadays tells you things you're familiar with, like Black women have problems. In a family situation, I'm talking about a classic, if you understand what I'm saying, a classic Black woman figure. Showing her not just surviving, yet surviving, not just being but being, but also not just being a slave but you know still being a slave, not just being a whole but just the Black woman in all her majesty. The Black woman in all her non-majesty as well. The Black woman surviving yet not surviving but being. If that makes any kind of sense.

II.
Plays

The Bronx Is Next

(1968)

CHARACTERS:

    CHARLES
    OLD SISTER
    LARRY
    ROLAND
    JIMMY
    WHITE COP
    BLACK BITCH

The scene is a block in Harlem—a block of tenement houses on either side of a long, narrow, dirty street of full garbage cans. People are moving around in the distance bringing things out of the houses and standing with them in the street. There is activity—but as CHARLES, a tall bearded man in his early thirties, and OLD SISTER move toward the front, the activity lessens. It is night. The time is now.

CHARLES: Keep 'em moving Roland. C'mon you mothafuckers. Keep moving. Git you slow asses out of here. We ain't got all night. Into the streets. Oh shit. Look sister. None of that. You can't take those things. Jest important things—things you would grab and carry out in case of a fire. You understand? You wouldn't have time to get all of those things if there was a real fire.

OLD SISTER: Yes son. I knows what you says is true. But you see them things is me. I brought them up with me from Birmingham 40 years ago. I always keeps them right here with me. I jest can't do without them. You know what I mean son? I jest can't leave them you see.

CHARLES: Yes sister. I know what you mean. Look. Someone will help you get back to your apartment. You can stay there. You don't have to come tonight. You can come some other time when we have room for your stuff. OK?

OLD SISTER:	Thank you son. Here let me kiss you. Thank the lord there is young men like you who still care about the old people. What is your name son?
CHARLES:	My name is Charles, sister. Now I have to get back to work. Hey Roland. Jimmy. Take this one back up to her apartment. Make her comfortable. She ain't coming tonight. She'll come another time.
ROLAND:	Another time? Man you flipping out? Why don't you realize. . . .
CHARLES:	I said, Roland, she'll come another time. Now help her up those fucking stairs. Oh yes. Jimmy, see too that she gets some hot tea. You dig? Ten o'clock is our time. There ain't no time for anyone. There ain't no time for nothing 'cept what we came to do. Understand? Now get your ass stepping.

(ROLAND and JIMMY exit.)

LARRY:	Hey Charles, over here fast. Look what I found coming out one of the buildings.
CHARLES:	What, man? I told you I ain't got no time for nothing 'cept getting this block cleared out by 10 p.m. What the fuck is it?
LARRY:	A white dude. A cop. An almighty fuzz. Look. I thought they were paid enough to stay out of Harlem tonight. *(Turns to COP)* Man. Now just what you doing here spying on us, huh?
WHITE COP:	Spying? What do you mean spying? You see. Well you know how it is. I have this friend—she lives on this block and when I got off at 4 p.m., I stopped by. Well, I was just leaving but this guy and another one taking someone upstairs saw me—pulled a gun on me and brought me out here.
CHARLES:	What building and what apartment were you visiting my man?
WHITE COP:	No. 214—Apt. 10—but why are you interested?
CHARLES:	Larry, bring the black bitch out fast. Want to get a good look at her so I'll see jest why we sweating tonight. Yeah. For all the black bitches like her.

WHITE COP:	*(Has turned around and seen the activity)* Hey. What are all the people doing out in the middle of the street? What's happening here? There's something going on here I don't know about and I have a right to know . . . .
CHARLES:	Right? Man. You ain't got no rights here. Jest shut your fucking white mouth before you git into something you wish you wasn't in. Man. I've got to call in about this dude. Is there a phone in any of these firetraps?
JIMMY:	Yeah. I got one in my place during the year I lived here. It's No. 210-1st floor-1C-back apartment. I'll stay here with this socializing dude while you call.

(CHARLES splits.)

WHITE COP:	*(Takes out some cigarettes)* Want a cigarette?
JIMMY:	Thanks man—in fact I'll take the whole pack. It's going to be a long night.
WHITE COP:	What do you mean a long night?
JIMMY:	*(Smiling)* Jest what I said man—and it might be your longest—*(laughs)*—maybe the longest of your life.
WHITE COP:	*(Puffing on cigarette—leans against garbage can)* What's your name son?
JIMMY:	You don't git nothing out of me 'til Charles returns. You hear me? So stop asking so many damn questions. *(Moves to the right. Screams)* Goddamn it Roland. Your building is going too slow. We have only two more hours. Get that shit moving. We have to be finished by 10 p.m.
WHITE COP:	Look. What are you people doing? Why are all the people moving out into the street—What's going on here? There's something funny going on here and I want to know what it is. You can't keep me from using my eyes and brains—and pretty soon I'll put two and two together—then you just wait . . . you just wait. . . .

(CHARLES has appeared on stage at this time and has heard what the COP has said. Is watchful for a moment—moves forward.)

| CHARLES: | Wait for what my man? Wait for you to find out what's happening? It's not hard to see. We're moving the people out— |

out into the cool breezes of the street—is that so difficult to understand?

WHITE COP: No. But why? I mean, yeah I know that the apartments are kinda hot and awful . . .

CHARLES: You right man. Kinda awful. Did you hear that description of these shit houses Jimmy? Kinda awful. I knew we weren't describing this scene right and it took this dude here to finally show us the way. From now on when I talk to people about their places I'll say—I know your places are kinda awful . . .

JIMMY: In fact, Charles, how 'bout—I know your places are maybe kinda awful . . .

CHARLES: (Laughing) Yeah. That's it. Perhaps. Maybe could there be a slight possibility that your place is kinda—now mind you, we ain't saying for sure—but maybe it's kinda awful—(becomes serious) Yeah. That's the white man for you man. Always understating things. But since both you and I know that these places are shit-houses, that conversation can end now.

JIMMY: What they say 'bout the dude, Charles?

CHARLES: (Turns to WHITE COP) Oh everything is cool. You can leave man when you want to, but first have a cigarette with us.

WHITE COP: (Relaxing) I would offer you some of mine, but he took them all.

CHARLES: C'mon man. Give them back to the dude. And Jimmy go get Roland. Tell him to come talk a bit. What a night this has been. It's hard working with these people. They like cattle you know. Don't really understand anything. Being a cop, you probably found that too. Right?

WHITE COP: (Lighting a cigarette) Yeah. I did. A little. But the hardest thing for me to understand was that all you black people would even live in these conditions. Well. You know. Everybody has had ghettoes, but they built theirs up and there was respect there. Here. There is none of that.

CHARLES: How right you are my man. C'mon in Jimmy and Roland. We just talking to pass some time. Of course, getting back to your statement, I think the reason that the black man

hasn't made it—you ain't Irish are you?—is a color thing—
I mean even though the Irish were poor they were still
white—but as long as white people hate because of a difference in color, then they ain't gonna let the black man do
too much. You dig?

WHITE COP: But all this hopelessness. Poverty of the mind and spirit.
Why? Things are so much better. All it takes is a little more
effort by you people. But these riots. It's making good people
have second thoughts about everything.

ROLAND: It's a long time going—man—this hopelessness—and it ain't
no better. Shit. All those good thinking people changing
their minds never believed in the first fucking place.

JIMMY: *(Stands up)* Man. Do you know that jest yesterday I was running down my ghetto street, and these two white dudes
stopped me and asked what I was doing out so early in
the morning—and cuz I was high off some smoke—I said
man—it's my street—I can walk on it any time. And they
grabbed me and told me where everything was.

CHARLES: That gives me an idea. Let's change places before this dude
splits. Let him be a black dude walking down a ghetto street,
and we'll be three white dudes—white cops on a Harlem
street.

WHITE COP: Oh c'mon. That's ridiculous. What good would that do. Why
I'd feel silly . . .

CHARLES: You mean you'd feel silly being black?

WHITE COP: Oh no—not that—I mean what would it prove? How would
it help—what good would it do?

JIMMY: But what harm could it do?

WHITE COP: None that I could imagine . . . it's just that it's strange . . . it's
like playing games.

ROLAND: Oh c'mon. I've always wanted to be a white dude—now's
my chance. It'll be exciting—sure is getting boring handling
this mob of people.

JIMMY: If you afraid, man, we don't have to.

WHITE COP: Afraid? No. OK. Let's start.

CHARLES: *(Jumps up—looks elated)* Then we'll jest be standing on the corner talking, and you c'mon by. Oh yeah, maybe you should be running. OK?

(CHARLES, ROLAND and JIMMY move to one side of the stage—the WHITE COP moves to the other side and begins to run toward them.)

CHARLES: Hey slow down boy. What's your hurry?

WHITE COP: *(Stops running)* Yes. What's wrong officer?

JIMMY: Where you running to so fast?

WHITE COP: I just felt like running officer. I was feeling good, so I decided to run.

ROLAND: Oh you were feeling good. So you decided to run. Now ain't that a load of shit if I ever heard one.

WHITE COP: It's true, officer. I was just thinking about the day—it was a great day for me so I felt like running—so I ran.

CHARLES: Boy! Who's chasing you? What did you steal?

WHITE COP: Steal? I haven't stolen anything. I haven't stolen anything. I haven't anything in my pockets. *(Goes into his pockets)*

JIMMY: *(Draws gun)* Get your hands out of your pockets boy. Against the wall right now.

WHITE COP: But what have I done? I was just running. This is not legal you know. You have no right to do this. . . .

ROLAND: You are perfectly correct. We have no right to do this. Why I even have no right to hit you, but I am. *(Hits WHITE COP with gun)*

WHITE COP: *(Falls down. Gets up)* Now wait a minute. That is going just a little too far and . . .

CHARLES: I said why were you running down that street boy?

WHITE COP: Look. Enough is enough. I'm ready to stop—I'm tired.

JIMMY: What's wrong nigger boy—can't you answer simple questions when you're asked them. Oh I know what's wrong. You need me to help you remember. *(Hits WHITE COP with gun)*

WHITE COP: Have you gone crazy? Stop this. You stop it now, or there will be consequences.

ROLAND: What did you steal black boy—we can't find it on you, but we know you got it hidden someplace. (*Hits him again*)

WHITE COP: Oh my god. Stop it . . . this can't be happening to me. Look— I'm still me. It was only make believe.

CHARLES: Let's take him in. He won't cooperate. He won't answer the question. Maybe he needs more help than the three of us are giving him.

JIMMY: I don't know. Looks like he's trying to escape to me. Take out your guns. That nigger is trying to run. Look at him. Boy, don't run. Stop. I say if you don't stop, I'll have to shoot.

WHITE COP: Are you all mad? I'm not running. I'm on my knees. Stop it. This can't continue. Why . . .

ROLAND: You ain't shit boy. You black. You a nigger we caught running down the street—running and stealing like all the niggers around him.

CHARLES: Now you trying to escape—we warned you three times already. You only get three warnings then . . . (*Noise from off stage—a woman's voice*)

LARRY: Man. This bitch ain't cooperating Charles. She said she didn't have to come. Finally had to slap her around a bit.

CHARLES: Now is that anyway to act, bitch? We just want to talk to you for a minute. Hear you were entertaining this white dude in your place. Is that so?

BLACK BITCH: (*Stands defiantly—has a reddish wig on, which is slightly disheveled*) Who you? Man. I don't owe no black man no explanation 'bout what I do. The last man I explained to cleaned me out, so whatever you doing don't concern me 'specially if it has a black man at the head.

JIMMY: Smart—assed—bitch.

BLACK BITCH: (*Turns to JIMMY—walks over to him*) That's right kid. A smart—assed—black bitch—that's me. Smart enough to stay clear of all black bastard men who jump from black pussy to black pussy like jumping jacks. Yeah, I know all about black men. The toms and the revolutionary ones. I could keep you entertained all night long. But I got to get back. My kids will be coming home.

CHARLES: How many kids you got bitch?

BLACK BITCH: Two. Two boys. Two beautiful black boys. Smart boys you hear? They read. They know more than me already, but they still love me. Men. They will know what a woman is for. I'll teach them. I ain't educated, but I'll say—hold them in your arms—love them—love your black woman always. I'll say I am a black woman and I cry in the night. But when you are men, you will never make a black woman cry in the night. You hear. And they'll promise.

ROLAND: Oh shit. Another black matriarch on our hands—and with her white boyfriend. How you gonna teach them all this great stuff when you whoring with some white dude who kills black men everyday? How you explain that shit to them?

BLACK BITCH: *(Laughs—high piercing laugh—walks over to WHITE COP)* Explain this? *(Points to WHITE COP on ground)* I only explain the important things. He comes once a week. He fucks me. He puts his grayish white dick in me and dreams his dreams. They ain't 'bout me. Explain him to my boys. *(Laughs)* Man. I am surviving. This dude has been coming regularly for two years—he stays one evening, leaves and then drives on out to Long Island to his white wife and kids and reality. *(Laughs)* Explain. I don't explain cuz there ain't nothing to explain.

CHARLES: Yeah. But you still a bitch. You know. None of this explaining to us keeps you from being a bitch.

BLACK BITCH: Yeah. I know what I am. *(Looks around)* But all you revolutionists or nationalists or whatever you call yourselves—do you know where you at? I am a black woman, and I've had black men who could not love me or my black boys—where you gonna find black women to love you when all this is over—when you need them? As for me I said no black man would touch me ever again.

CHARLES: *(Moving toward the BLACK BITCH)* Is that right? You not a bad looking bitch if you take off that fucking wig. *(Throws it off)* A good ass. *(Touches her face, neck, moves his hands on her body—moves against her until she tries to turn away)* No don't turn away bitch. Kiss me. I said kiss me. *(Begins to kiss her face—slowly—sensuously—the BLACK BITCH grabs him and kisses him long and hard—moves her body against him.)* Yeah. No black man could touch you again, huh? *(Laughs and moves away)* I could fuck you right here if I wanted to. You know what a black man is don't you bitch? Is that what happens when you fuck faggoty white men?

(BLACK BITCH runs across the stage and with that run and cry that comes from her she grabs CHARLES and hits him and holds on. CHARLES turns and knocks her down. The white dude turns away. Jimmy moves toward her.)

BLACK BITCH: No. Watch this boy. You still young. Watch me. Don't touch me. Watch me get up. It hurts. But I'll get up. And when I'm up the tears will stop. I don't cry, when I'm standing up. All right. I'm up again. Who else? Here I am, a black bitch, up for grabs. Anyone here for me? Take your choice—your pick— slap me or fuck me—anyway you get the same charge.

JIMMY: Here black bitch. Let me help you. Your eye is swollen. *(Doesn't look at CHARLES)* Can she go back to her place and get some things out Charles? I'll help her.

CHARLES: You have five minutes to help the black bitch then get your black ass back here. We wasted enough time. *(Stoops)* Here don't forget her passport to the white world. *(Throws wig at her)* And keep your mouth shut black bitch. You hear?

BLACK BITCH: *(Putting on her wig)* I told you I only explain important things. There ain't nothing happening here yet that's important to me.

(Exits with JIMMY)

CHARLES: *(Laughs)* That's a woman there. Yeah wig and all. She felt good for awhile. Hey you. Dude. You can get up now. All the unpleasantness is over. Here let me help you get cleaned up. *(Begins to brush WHITE COP off)* We just got a little carried away with ourselves.

WHITE COP:	Can I go now? I'm tired. It's been a long night. You said I could go.
CHARLES:	But don't you want to go and see the bitch—see how she is—make sure she's okay?
WHITE COP:	No. I don't think so. It's late. My wife will be worrying by now.
CHARLES:	Isn't there anything else you want to see before you go? Can't I fill you in on anything?
WHITE COP:	I've seen people moved into the street. That's all. Nothing else. I want to know nothing.
CHARLES:	Would you believe that it's happening on every street in Harlem?
WHITE COP:	*(Nervously)* I'm not interested. I just want to leave and go home. I'm tired.
CHARLES:	Yeah man. You look tired. Look. Do me a favor. I want to go to the bitch's place and apologize. You know it wasn't right. Hurting her like that. Come with me. Hey Roland. Shouldn't he come with me?
ROLAND:	Yeah man. He should. After all, he knows her better than you. He can tell you what approach to use with her.
WHITE COP:	No. I don't want to go. I don't want to see her again. It's all finished now. I'm tired. You tell her. Just let me go on home.
CHARLES:	But man. I need you. I need you to help me talk to her. She'll listen to you. Anyway with you there, you'll keep me from getting violent again—c'mon man. Just this one thing then you can go.
LARRY:	*(Larry's voice from off stage)* We ready to light, Charles—should we start now?
CHARLES:	Yeah. All 'cept No. 214—we have some business there. Give us ten minutes then light it up. *(WHITE COP tries to run— CHARLES and ROLAND grab his arm and start walking.)*
WHITE COP:	I don't want to go. I must get home. My wife and two boys are waiting for me. I have never hurt or killed a black person

in my life. Yes. I heard talk that some cops did—that they hated black people—but not me. I listened. It made me sick, but I never participated in it. I didn't ever do anything to Negroes. No. I don't want to go. I haven't done anything. *(Begins to cry)* Holy Mother—you can't do this to me. *(Screams)* But, I'm white! I'm white! No. This can't be happening— I'm white! *(Tries to break away and ROLAND knocks him out— they pull him off stage. The stage becomes light—buildings are burning—people are moving around looking at the blaze. JIMMY, ROLAND and CHARLES reappear.)*

JIMMY: Well. That's that, man. What a night. Do I still have to write this up tonight, Charles?

CHARLES: Were those your orders?

JIMMY: Yes. Okay. I'll do it while we wait. I'll drop it in the mailbox tonight. See you soon.

CHARLES: A good job, Jimmy. Stay with them. Talk to them. They need us more than ever now.

ROLAND: We got to split Charles. We got a meeting going tonight. You know what the meeting is about man? *(Takes out a cigarette)* You think this is the right strategy burning out the ghettoes? Don't make much sense to me man. But orders is orders. You know what's going down next?

CHARLES: *(Lighting a cigarette)* Yeah. I heard tonight when I called about that white dude. The Bronx is next—Let's split.

Sister Son/ji

(1969)

CHARACTER:	SISTER SON/JI
	dressed in shapeless blk/burlap, blk/leotards & stockings; gray/ natural wig—is made to look in her fifties.
SCENE:	*The stage is dark except for a light directed on the middle of the stage where there is a dressing/room/table with drawers/and chair—a noise is heard off stage—more like a deep/guttural/ laugh mixed with the sound of two/slow/dragging feet—as a figure moves and stops, back to the audience, the stage lightens.*
TIME:	*Age and now and never again.*

SISTER SON/JI: *(As she turns around, the faint sound of music is heard.)* not yet. turn off that god/damn music, this is not my music/day. i'll tell u when to play music to soothe my savage sounds. this is my quiet time, my time for reading or thinking thoughts that shd be thought *(pause)* now after all that talk, what deep thoughts shd i think today. Shall they be deeper than the sounds of my blk/today or shall they be louder than the sounds of my white/yesterdays. *(Moves to the dressing/ table and sits in the chair)* Standing is for young people. i ain't young no mo. My young days have gone, they passed me by so fast that i didn't even have a chance to see them. What did i do with them? What did i say to them? do i still remember them? Shd I remember them? hold on Sister Son/ji—today is tuesday. Wed. is yr/day for remembering. tuesday is for reading and thinking thoughts of change.

Hold on! hold on for what? am i not old? older than the mississippi hills i settled near. Ain't time and i made a truce so that i am time

a blk/version of past/ago & now/time.

no, if i want to i shall remember.

rememberings are for the old.

What else is left them? My family is gone. all my beautiful children are buried here in mississippi.

Chausiku. Mtume. Baraka. Mungu./brave warriors. DEAD.

Yes. rememberings are for the near/dead/dying.

for death is made up of past/actions/deeds and thoughts. (Rises)

So. Fuck the hold/ons today. i shall be a remembered Sister Son/ji. today i shall be what i was/shd have been and never can be again. today i shall bring back yesterday as it can never be today.

as it should be tomorrow. (She drags her chair back to the dressing table and opens the drawer—her movements are still slow-oldish—she takes off her gray/wig and puts on a straightened blk/wig—stands and puts on a wide belt, a long necklace and a bracelet on her right ankle. As she sits and begins to remove the make/up of old age from her face her movements quicken and become more active. A recording of Sammy Davis Jr. singing, "This is my beloved" is heard and she joins in.)

SISTER SON/JI: "strange spice from the south, honey from the dew drifting, imagine this in one perfect one and this is my beloved. And when he moves and when he talks to me, music—ah-ah-mystery—"

(Hums the rest as she takes off all the make/up and puts on some lipstick. When she stands again she is young—a young/negro/woman of 18 or 19. She picks up a note/book and begins to run across the stage.)

SISTER SON/JI: i'm coming nesbitt. i'm coming. Hey. thought i'd never catch u—how are u? (Looks down for she has that shyness of very young women who are unsure/uncertain of themselves and she stretches out her hand and begins to walk—a lover's walk.) yeah, i'm glad today is friday too. that place is a mad/house. hunter college indeed. do u know nesbitt that that ole/bitch in my political theory course couldn't remember my name and there are only 12 of us in the class—only 3 negroes—as different as day and night and she called out Miss Jones, Miss Smith, Miss Thomas and each time she looked at the three of us and couldn't remember who was who. Ain't that a drag? But she remembered the ofays' names/faces and they all look like honey. *(Turns and faces him)* you know what i did? u know what i did nesbitt? i stood up, picked up my note/book and headed for the door and u know she asked where i was going and i said out of here—away from u because u don't even know my name unless i raise my hand when u spit out three/blk/names— and she became that flustered/red/whiteness that ofays become, and said but u see it's just that—and i finished it for her—i sd it's just that we all look alike. yeah. well damn this class (I wanted to say fuck this class, honey, but she might have had a heart/attack/rt/there in class) i said damn this class. i'm a human being to be remembered just like all these other human beings in this class. and with that I walked out. *(Is smiling as she turns her head)* what did u say? am i going back? no honey. how/why shd i return? she showed me no respect. none of the negroes in that class was being respected as the individuals we are. just three/ big/blk/masses of blk/womanhood. that is not it. can't be. *(Stops walking)* Uh-huh. i'll lose the credit for that course but i'll appeal when i'm a senior and u know what i'll write on that paper. i'll write the reason i lost these three credits is due to discrimination, yes, that's what i'll say and . . . oh honey. yes. it might have been foolish but it was right. after all at some point a person's got to stand up for herself just a little and . . . oh. u have a surprise. what? there? that's yrs? boss. o it's boss. *(Jumps up and down)* Nesbitt yr/father is the nicest man. what a beautiful car. now u can drive up from Howard on weekends. yes. i'd like that. Let's go for a ride, u know upstate N.Y. is pretty this time of yr. where we headed for?

Yes i do love u nesbitt. i've told u so many times but i'm scared to do it because I might get pregnant; i'm scared of the act, i guess u're right in saying that i'm against it becuz it has not been sanctioned by church/marriage and

i'm trembling nesbitt.
i feel the cold air on my thighs. how shall I move my
   love; i keep missing the beat of yr/fast/movements.

is it time to go already? that's rt. we do have to go to
  yr/father's/dance. how do i look?
any different? i thought not. i'm ready to go.

(Softly) nesbitt do u think after a first love each succeeding
love is a repetition? *(The stage darkens and SON/JI moves to
the dressing table and sits. Then a tape of Malcolm's voice is
heard and SON/JI adds a long skirt, removes the straightened/
wig and puts on large/hoop/earrings.)*

SISTER SON/JI: racist? brothers & sisters. he is not the racist here in white/
america. he is a beautiful/blk/man who talks about sepa-
ration cuz we must move there. no more fucking SIT/ins-
toilet/ins-EAT/ins—just like he says—the time for ins is over
and the time for outs is here. out of this sadistic/masoch-
istic/society that screams its paleface over the world. the
time for blk/nationhood is here. *(Gets up and moves forward)*

Listen. listen. did u hear those blk/words of that
  beautiful/blk/warrior/prince—

Did u see his flashing eyes and did u hear his dagger/words.
cuz if u did then u will know as i have come to know. u will
change—u will pick up yr/roots and become yr/self again—
u will come home to blk/ness for he has looked blk/people
in the eye and said

welcome home. yr/beautiful/blkness/awaits u. here's my
hand brother/sister—welcome. Home. *(Stage lightens)*

brother Williams, this blk/power/conference is outa sight. i
ain't never seen so many heavee/blk/people together. i am
learning too much. this morning i heard a sister talk about
blk/women supporting their blk/men, listening to their
men, sacrificing, working while blk/men take care of bizness, having warriors and young sisters. i shall leave this
conference brother with her words on my lips. i will talk
to sisters abt loving their blk/men and letting them move
in tall/straight/lines toward our freedom. yes i will preach
blk/love/respect between blk/men and women for that will
be the core/basis of our future in white/america.

But, why do u have to split man. u've been out all this week
to meetings. can't we have some time together. the child is

in bed. and i don't feel like reading. it's just 11P.M. can't we talk/touch. we hardly talk anymore. i'm afraid that one day we'll have nothing to say to each other.

yes. i know u're tired. i know that the brothers are always on yr/case where u're organizing; and u need to unwind from the week but i want to unwind with u. i want to have a glass of wine with u and move into yr/arms; i want to feel u moving inside of me. we haven't made love in weeks man and my body feels dead, unalive. i want to talk abt our past/future—if we have one in this ass/hole country. Don't go. Stay home with me and let us start building true blk/lives—let our family be a family built on mutual love and respect. Don't leave me man. i've been by myself for weeks. we need time together. blk/people gots to spend all their spare time together or they'll fall into the same traps their fathers and mothers fell into when they went their separate ways and one called it retaining their manhood while the other called it just plain/don't/care/about/family/hood. a man is a man in a house where a woman/children cry out for a man's presence—where young warriors can observe their father's ways and grow older in them—where young sisters can receive the smiles of their fathers and carry their smiles to their future husbands. Is there time for all this drinking—going from bar to bar. Shouldn't we be getting ourselves together—strengthening our minds, bodies and souls away from drugs, weed, whiskey and going out on Saturday nites. alone. what is it all about or is the rhetoric apart from the actual being/doing? What is it all about if the doings do not match the words?

(The stage becomes dark with only a spotlight on SISTER SON/JI's face and since she is constantly moving on the stage, sometimes she is not seen too clearly.)

SISTER SON/JI: *(Is crooning softly)* hee. haa haa. THE HONKIES ARE COMING TO TOWN TODAY. HOORAY. HOORAY. HOORAY.

THE CRACKERS ARE COMING TO TOWN TODAY. TODAY. TODAY. HOORAY.

where are u man? hee hee hee. the shadow knows. we are our brother's keepers. we must have an undying love for each other.

it's 5 A.M. in the morning.
i am scared of voices moving in my head.
ring-around-the-honkies-a-pocketful-of-
    gunskerboomkerboomwehavenopains.

the child is moving inside of me. where are you? Man yr/son moves against this silence. he kicks against my silence.

Aaaaaaah. Aaaaaaah. Aaaaaaah. oh, i must keep walking. man, come fast. come faster than the speed of bullets— faster that the speed of lightning and when u come we'll see it's SUPER-BLOOD. HEE HEE. HAA. FOOLED U DIDN'T IT? Ahh—go way. go way voices that send me spinning into nothingness. Ah. aah. aaah. aaaaah. Aaaaaah. aAaaAaah. Aaaaah. Aaaaaah. AaAaah. AaaaaaaaaaaaaaaaaaaaaH. (SIS-TER SON/JI falls on her knees and chants.)

What is my name o blk/prince in what house do
I walk while i smell yr/distant smells
how have i come into this land
by what caravan did i cross the
desert of yr/blk/body?

(SISTER SON/JI finally moves to dressing/table. Her walk is slower, almost oldish. She rests her head. Then the sound of drums is heard mixed with a Coltrane sound. SISTER SON/JI puts her hands over her ears to drown out the sounds but they grow louder and she lifts her head, removes her jewelry, removes the long skirt, puts on a gun and belt, ties a kerchief around her head and puts a baby/carrier on her back. The music subsides.)

SISTER SON/JI: do u think they will really attack us? what abt world opin-ion? no, i hadn't noticed that they had a new administra-tion, newer and better fascist pigs. So we must send all the children away. will i help take them? but will i have enough time to get back and help. good. Ahh—u think it'll be a long/drawn/out fight. are we well prepared, mume?— come children. Malika-Nakawa-Damisi, Mungu, Mjumbe, Mtume, Baraka. come. the trucks are ready to take us on our trip. make sure u have yr/lunches and canteens. make sure u have yr/identification tags, where is our drummer?

Mwenge play us yur/songs as we leave.

i shall return soon, mume. i shall return soon. (The sounds of guns/helicopters are heard.)

So the war is becoming unpopular, and many devils are refusing to fight us. good. mume, can we trust the devils who have come to fight on our side? the women and I don't mind the male/devils here but the female/devils who have followed them. they shd not be allowed here. what happens to them when the one they are following is killed. It will become a problem if we don't send them packing rt away.

Ah, that sounds like a heavy attack. It is. women, sisters. Let us sing the killing/song for our men. let us scream the words of dying as we turn/move against the enemy.

(SISTER SON/JI moves as she chants.)

OOOOU-WAH
OOOOU-WAH
OOOU-OOOU-OOOU-WAH-WAH-WAH-
OOOU-OOOU-OOOU-WAH-WAH-WAH-
EEYE-YO
EEYE-YO
EEYE-EEYE-EEYE-YO-YO-
EEYE-EEYE-EEYE-YO-YO-

Is it true that Mungu is here? But, he is only thirteen. a child. He's still a child, mume. He's as tall as u mume but he's still a boy. send him back. all the other warriors are fifteen. are we—do we need soldiers that badly. Mume, please send him back. he's just a boy. he's just my little boy. he's not so tall stretched out on the ground. the bullets have taken away his height. Mungu, Mungu, Mungu. can u hear me? do my words go in and out yr/bullet/holes till they finally rest inside u? Mungu. Mungu. Mungu. My first warrior. i love u my little one even as u stare yr/death stare.

(SCREAM—HEY—SCREAM—HEY.)

Yes. u, death. i'm calling yr/name. why not me? Stay away from my family. i've given u one son—one warrior for yr/apprenticeship. git stepping death for our tomorrows will be full of life/living/births.

if he keeps the devil/woman then he shd be made to leave. Yes. he must go. Mume, tell me what are all these deaths for, with more likely to come? so he can feel sorry for a devil/woman and bring her whiteness among all this BLK/NESS.

he feels sorry for her. and what abt our teachings. have we forgotten so soon that we hate devils. that we are in a death/struggle with the beasts. if she's so good, so liberal, send her back to her own kind. Let her liberalize them. Let her become a camp follower to the hatred that chokes white/america. yes I wd vote to send yr/partner to certain death if he tries to keep her.

these mississippi hills will not give up our dead. my son/ our son did not die for integration. u must still remember those ago/yrs when we had our blk/white period. they died for the right of blk/children to run on their own land and let their bodies explode with the sheer joy of living. of being blk/and many children have died and these brown hills and red gullies will not give up our dead. and neither will i. (*The sounds of guns, planes are heard. SISTER SON/JI moves slowly to the dressing/table. The war/sounds decrease and a sound like Coltrane mixed with drums begin slowly, tiredly. She puts on the gray/haired/wig, takes off the gun and baby carrier—and puts on the make/up of all the yrs she has gathered. Then she turns around in the chair and stares at the audience.*)

SISTER SON/JI: Death is a five o'clock door forever changing time. And wars end. Sometimes too late. i am here. still in mississippi. Near the graves of my past. We are at peace. the state supports me and others like me and i have all the time i want to do what all old/dying people do. Nothing. but I have my memories. (*Rises*) Yes. hee, hee. i have my sweet/astringent memories becuz we dared to pick up the day and shake its tail until it became evening. a time for us. blk/ness. blk/people. Anybody can grab the day and make it stop. can u my friends? or maybe it's better if i ask: WILL YOU?

Dirty Hearts

(1971)

PERSONS: FIRST MAN
             SECOND MAN
             SHIGEKO
             CARL
             THE POET

(Two men are sitting at a table playing cards. They are neither young nor old. There are three empty chairs around the table. The lighting is dim.)

FIRST MAN: *(Throwing the cards across the table petulantly)* I don't like it. let's wait for them. i don't like to play cards with one person; everything is known then. i like the suspense of crowds when i play. where are they today? i don't like to be kept waiting. *(Rises and lights a cigarette)* that was one of the irritating qualities Helen had—always late *(laughs)*—even in sex. the night i decided to leave, she had a hysterical orgasm—the first one we had ever had together; if you'll excuse the fabricated ones she had before we were married. years togetha and she never once enjoyed touching my body swollen with love.

SECOND MAN: *(Still holding his cards, but concentrating on the room)* today—have you noticed that today is quiet. extraordinarily quiet. listen. there's no noise coming from the streets. there's something different. i don't exactly know. like a yellow contagion left over from the nite. a quarantine of kind. some permanent isolation invading our world. don't you feel it?

FIRST MAN: *(Looking scornfully at SECOND MAN)* sometimes i think i am a fool to live with you, a fool in search of perpetual frolic. i did not leave my wife, i did not walk out of that nest of congruity—from that female institute of intuition—yes, one wife and three gangling girls—to listen to this drivel that leaks from your conscience. *(Walks to the window)* it is only cloudy today. i would say that it's cloudy on the average of once a week, and this week is no different from any other.

(A girl enters the room. She wears a print dress and a beach hat that covers most of her face. She sits in a chair, her back to the audience.)

FIRST MAN: hello, Shigeko. you're first. everyone is late. did you have much to do today? is she working you very hard?

SHIGEKO: *(Speaking English slowly and hesitantly)* no, your wife had no need of me today. she said she wanted to be alone. i left the house early—i wanted to walk, i wanted to feel this city, the pavement pressed by thousands of people, under my feet. i felt very sad; i felt as if i had forgotten something, but i did not know what it was; so i had no place to go. i miss perhaps my beautiful, leveled country.

SECOND MAN: *(Jokingly)* walking among these leisured ruins is not protocol for a young girl, Shigeko.

FIRST MAN: *(Looking meaningfully at second man while moving toward SHI-GEKO)* i know exactly what you mean, Shigeko. you are lonely, but listen to it while it lasts. loneliness selects the sensitive people, the people who care and feel all the stupid faces of the world staring. . . if your work is too tiring, i'll find you another position, something easier since you are now in school.

SHIGEKO: *(Apologetically)* everything is fine, everything is all right, everything. all has been reduced to its simplest terms for me. you are a kind man. america is kind, it's merely that today, something about this day *(hands move nervously)* that makes me want to keep moving—to run and talk to strangers.

SECOND MAN: *(Sitting forward)* you feel it also, this blanket covering the day? is there noise outside? isn't there an active quiet about us, and isolated virus where you have been?

FIRST MAN: will you please shut the hell up or get out. *(Turns to SHI-GEKO)* take off that hat, you don't need it here. let's start the game.

(SHIGEKO rises—removes her hat and takes a chair facing the

audience. Her face is heavily made-up—but from the nose downwards the face is disfigured.)

i am tired of waiting for the others.

SECOND MAN: *(Picking up cards and beginning to shuffle; repeating softly)*

where you have been . . . where you have been . . .
(Looks at SHIGEKO)
i have been amid organized death that hurried
i have been at

SHIGEKO: *(Softly)*

sea among charitable waves
i have been forgotten by those who once knew me
i have been alone.
i have been under bleached skies that dropped silver
i have been open flesh replaced by commemorative
    crusts
i have been taped.
i have been specific among generalities
i have been fed residual death in a bottle
i have been mourning for sterile faces
i have been obliged.

FIRST MAN: if you two have ceased your negative reminiscences, perhaps we can begin.

SHIGEKO: *(Quietly)* i feel no bitterness, you know. i said those words an evening long ago when i was still sensitive about people staring. when i saw you looking, i had been remembering the past, when i used to run on my own hill in my country—i was racing the skies and singing to the blossoms

that blessed our war-torn land; and my face tingled with the day's color and my blood young and life. i was angry because you made me remember. i am not bitter now. you did not know what would happen—you didn't do it—it was someone else who made the decisions—removed from you. i am grateful to be alive.

(The doors open and a Black man enters. He carries a briefcase, bulging with papers. Cool drops of sweat pour from his head as he falls into the chair—his back is to the audience.)

FIRST MAN: well, Carl, it's about time. you will have to delegate some of your responsibilities. this is the second time this week you've been late. but now, we can start the game.

(A game begins. It is called Dirty Hearts. All of the cards are dealt out. Each person plays his cards slowly and as the cards diminish a slight tension develops among the players until each one separately looks at CARL. Then the FIRST MAN slaps a card on the table triumphantly.)

CARL: why me again, today? i received the queen of spades yesterday. i don't deserve it. you had a chance to give it to both of them—but you waited like the controlled . . . *(pause)* i am finished. i don't want to play this childish game. i have too many important things to think about. *(Rises)*

FIRST MAN: well—then perhaps we will discontinue playing your childish game of "who am I today?"

CARL: *(Turning excitedly)* what do you mean? everyone here knows who, what i am. i am a blk/capitalist. i am the president of Lanson and Company. i am in control of a company. i worked my way up from a stock clerk, yes a stock clerk, to the top. i am the american way of life; i am the american dream. *(Picks up his briefcase)* you see these papers— contracts, decisions to be made—people to meet and persuade to deal with me—trips to be made—schedules to follow. all of this i am—powerful, by hard work, constant ambition, constant awareness that the company needed me and *(sits down)* wanted me. *(Pause)* where are the refreshments today? i think we need a drink. *(Moves over to bar and fixes a drink)* this day is strange. i've had the feeling today that if i screamed no one would hear me, not that i entertained any such nonsense, but it is as if we are playing records and no music is heard.

SECOND MAN: *(Almost to himself)* yes, i know. i feel it and i haven't been outside, in fact, not since the last time. but, it is here again. three months ago it was like this also. what will save us today?

CARL: *(Glass in hand; sitting down to face the audience)* i had a dream last night. the first dream i have ever had or remembered. i was in a strange place—a southern town and i was picked up for vagrancy by the police. they took me to their country club for questioning. then i was released and escorted to a dining room. two waiters brought food and when i asked for silverware they laughed and the lights grew dim. they repeated this many times until the policemen came and took me to a hotel. there i filled out a card and gave it to a clerk who looked at me and threw the card away saying "it says where do you come from boy. write the truth." i repeated i am from N.Y. City. this continued until the discarded cards began to circle the room, drawing near me, suffocatingly. i screamed you dirty crackers—all of you— *(rises)* you dirty crackers, listen and laugh. *(Pause)*

> i come from white shadows that hide my indigence
> i come from waking streets that are detoured
> i come from pushing wagons that do not turn
> i come from indifference.
> i come from uncut cloth that patterns me
> i come from vague violets, gift wrapped by slum-
> > parked
>
> thoughts
> i come from hate
> i come from men who assume no responsibilities
> i come from their wives who claw in the darkness
> i come from white spit foaming with militant bubbles
> i come from hell.

then they came toward me and beat me over, and over, and over. and i laughed until my body began to shake with the knowledge that they couldn't hurt me and i laughed & rolled on the floor until it divided, was separated. and the cuts began to heal miraculously. and still i laughed. each day I looked at them from my side and laughed until i was a boy again. *(Sits down and begins to laugh softly)*

(The FIRST MAN rises, genuinely moved, and pats CARL on the back.)

FIRST MAN: *(Meditatively)* yes, we all dream for our analysts. i dreamed last night that i had a villa in italy. i was waiting for someone. and ten years passed. the servants were eunuchs; and one remained with me at all times. i had peace, quiet, and protection anyone would envy. one night she came. she wore a blue chiffon gown that smelled of garden flowers. we loved the night into day. when I awoke she was gone and I cried in rage as i saw the young leaves falling from the trees. *(Pause)* it is funny—i remember the servants were smiling and their smiling faces grew larger & larger each year.

(During the above, the POET enters the room and listens. He leans against the door.)

POET: if we lived our feelings we would not have to dream among cloistered rooms *(smiles)* although i live a constant dream, but poets are always alone, or lonely, while they put life at rhythmic ease. *(Pause)* however i came to say that i cannot stay. i am at work on a poem concerning the aegean sea.

SECOND MAN: you write of seas, pianos and paintings that have had their say. i remember you used to write about life and people and flowers bent against the sky. are we so horrible now that you turn to dead things?

POET: i write about old things, past things, perhaps dead things because i am dead and at ease with my contemporaries. i no longer write about you—or Shigeko or Carl. you are the world's painful propaganda. my legends are tried and true. do u know i have discovered a new myth. her name is Masturbas. i have an outline for a long poem. i can make her beauty from the past. the one true beauty. i see her face as i tour my rooms. i touch her face as we kiss & we are one. happy, i return to this world breathing the past's ancient fumes. then i can sleep. *(Pause)* i must go. but, before i go, since we are reflecting today, i will tell u where i am going in young words. in words i said once long ago. *(Laughs)* remember, i was drunk one nite. bloody drunk. i had just returned from jail. and we were celebrating my triumphant display of humanity over the bestiality of our society. suddenly i was tired and attempted to leave and when i was asked where i was going *(laughs)* especially since there was no place for me to go to, i turned and said archly:

> i am going among neutral clouds unpunctured
> i am going among men unpolished

i am going to museums unadorned
i am going home.
i am going to change congenital poverty
i am going to hold young heads in my hands and turn
    them
slowly
i am going to cry.
i am going amid striped weaves forever winding
i am going unstyled into a cave
i am going in the blue rain that drowns green crystals
i am going to die.

(Pauses) well enough of me and young dreams. i shall return tomorrow when the nites suspend their images and the day falls like a copper penny on my old face. for the days bring reality of friends, hellos, eating & digesting food, while the nites receive the tears of disillusioned old men who have lost themselves among unseeing sights. *(Exits)*

FIRST MAN: well he had another good load on. i wonder who has recently rejected his plea of love. come let's play another hand. we have time. *(Shuffles the cards and the game begins.)*

(The game proceeds as the other. There is little excitement in the beginning but when the cards diminish the FIRST MAN gives the queen of spades to CARL. CARL looks. Then he begins to laugh. He picks up his cards. Looks and laughs again. He rises and falls on the floor laughing.)

FIRST MAN: come Carl. can't you take a joke? i knew you didn't expect it again today and i couldn't resist the temptation. you should have seen the look on your face. why . . .

(CARL continues to laugh)

SHIGEKO: please Carl. stop. we'll play bridge. i know how u like to play. we'll be partners again & bid seven no trump. *(Pause)* please stop your laughter. it doesn't help. we'll play bridge and beat them unmercifully. please Carl— *(CARL continues to laugh.)*

FIRST MAN: *(Turning to SECOND MAN)* well say something. u are always talking. do something. he's hysterical. maybe a dunk or a slap . . .

SECOND MAN: *(Holding his cards, singing)*

> sometimes I feel like a motherless child
> sometimes I feel like a motherless child
> sometimes I feel like a motherless child
> a long way from home sweet home
> a long way from home. *(Continues to hum softly)*

(FIRST MAN rises and bends to pick up CARL. CARL pulls away, still slightly laughing. He turns around and picks up his brief-case, moves toward the door. He turns reeling.)

CARL: listen u dirty crackers, all of you, u dirty crackers. listen and laugh. you hear me. listen and laugh. i am an ex-social worker. now i own a furniture store. a goddamn ordinary furniture store and nothing else. *(Exits)*

(A loud shriek is heard from the streets. It is CARL. Then other noises appear and his scream is dissolved by the everyday noises now entering the room. The room lightens.)

SECOND MAN: *(Softly)* and we offer human employment to those who have known so little humanity. *(Turns to SHIGEKO)* what will u become Shigeko? a doctor, or a tender nurse in white?

SHIGEKO: *(Softly)* i think i shall become a nurse and treat new wounds already closing. i will give the medication of blue winds that stir dead tissues. i will bring love to man & spread its carriage over the universe until we forget the clouds & taste the sweet rain.

SECOND MAN: *(Softly)* we will not know u when you come.

FIRST MAN: ignore him Shigeko. imagine that from Carl. *(Pause)* & all because of a little joke. well i have an appointment with a beautiful lady. i'll see u home Shigeko. *(Rises and begins to ready himself. Turns to SECOND MAN)* i won't come in tonight. we will talk tomorrow. & stop looking your ex-cess of pity and sorrow. we did not make the world & her numerous problems. Carl is weak. i can't tolerate weak people. they make me nauseous. one of the most irritating qualities Helen had was her ability to feel sorry for people & to blame herself constantly for their predicaments. *(Has completed his grooming)* let's go Shigeko.

SHIGEKO: *(Putting on her hat; turning to SECOND MAN)* i'll see u satur-day. maybe saturday will not bring the drumming of neg-ligence. perhaps i will bring a funny story that will pierce these rooms. goodbye. *(Exits)*

SECOND MAN: *(Sitting and listening)* no, it is not today, perhaps tomorrow, we will feel completely this conquering order. not today. the screams of the earth were once constant. what happened? now no one screams. hardly ever. will there be someone tomorrow to break the quiet? who is left now? *(Pause)* who is left now besides the egoists? who is left now besides the breathers of forward lives who leave the noise of mankind bottled on a distant shore? who is left now besides the sit-ters? *(Rises. Goes to the window. Turns toward chair. Then sud-denly exits)*

(Nine people pass on the stage in rows of threes. Three are = to SHIGEKO, three to CARL, three to the POET. They circle the stage, turn and look at the audience, and exit. Two men enter the room. They are neither young nor old.)

Malcolm/Man Don't Live Here No Mo

(1972)

*(For Anita, Morani and Mungu Weusi and
the children at Liberation School, Pittsburgh, Penn.)*

CHARACTERS:	CHORUS (3 SISTUHS) BROTHA (about 14 or 15) SISTUH (bout 12, 13, or 14)
TIME:	NOW

SETTING:

*The children enter
snappen fingers to lines:
we a baddDDD people, we
a baddDDD people, and
as they form an X, they
repeat (2 times)*

*Don Lee's poem
"Black people are moving
moving to return this
earth into the hands of
human beings"*

3 SISTUHS:

we be's hero/worshippers
we be's death/worshippers
we be's leader/worshippers
BUT: we should be blk/people worshippers
AND: some of us are leaderless toooooday
our homes are emptee cuz
MALCOM/MAN DON'T LIVE HERE NO MO
MALCOM/MAN DON'T LIVE HERE NO MO

(to the tune of blue/bird blue bird thru my window)

Malcolm, Malcolm where did u come from
Malcolm, Malcolm where did u come from
Malcolm, Malcolm where did u come from
we neeeeeEED to know

(hums softly moven back to X)

SISTUH:

(holden/rocken baby in her arms. steps out to talk)
(malcolm's mother)

look at my sonNNN

look at my beautiful one
look at his red hair
on his head right there
ah how he smiles at me
how he looks. what does he see?
what do u see malcolm little
as I rock u a little?
in my arms & the evening beams
caress u & yo/dreams.

BROTHA: yes. teacher. I want to be just that—

(steps out a young malcolm x)

a lawyer. u say no cuz my skin's black
but my white/teacher say i'm real smart
i can do anything that i start.
why oh why am i patted on the head
like an animal who is well/fed.
why oh why am i discouraged to be
what i want and know can be me. me. Me
no. i'm not an uppity nigger
mr/white/teacher it's just hard to figger
why a small/blk/boy like me
is never encouraged to BE—
guess school ain't for me after all
guess i'll just have a ball
play around/jive/hurt my kind
cuz school done kicked me in the behind.

CHORUS, 3 SISTUHS: malcolm, malcolm where did u go?
malcolm, malcolm where did u go?
malcolm, malcolm where did u go?
weeeeeEEE want to know.

SISTUH: my name is wite/woman/amurica

(wite amurica)

u know what i be here for
c'mon malcolm, bad malcolm. man
check me out. love me while u can.
i'll give you a gun, dope, high living
u can be baddDDD cuz i'll be giving

u whiskey, reefers, wite women & hate
so c'mon malcolm let's u & me mate.

BROTHA: i'm a baddDDD nigguh from the mid-west

(older malcolm)

c'mon anyone—give me a test
Harlem ain't nothing. cuz I'm Big Red
if u don't like it i'll go upside yo/head.
don't like nobody. don't trust no one
my only friend is me & my gun
don't believe in no nigguhs. they's all to be had
& had they will be cuz i'm real baddDDD.
done split from Harlem got a chick who's ofay
we gonna pull a big big job today
we gonna be rich nigguhs in the USA
we gonna be big time. yea. yea. yea.

CHORUS, 3 SISTUHS: malcolm, malcolm where did u go to?
malcolm, malcolm where did u go to?
malcolm, malcolm where did u go to?
we wannnnnT to know.

SISTUH: my name is wite/justice for the poor

(wite/amurica carrying am/ flag & confederate flag)

so we gonna take u thru this door
of prison. where all BAD nigguhs go
to be part of an american show.
go on u bad nigguh in that cell
u don gone got caught & fell
heh. heh. HEH look at u now.
u a bad nigguh but we got u anyhow.

BROTHA: Prison. i'll die right here. oh i'll die.

(prisoner/malcolm)

don't know what to do feel like i'll cry
who that. what's that i see. a light
sayen that blackness is right?
yes I submit to u O MESSENGER
you have told me who's our oppressor

yes I submit to u Elijah, a black/man
who will give blk/people their land.

CHORUS, 3 SISTUHS: malcolm malcolm, how are u do/en
malcolm malcolm, how are u do/en
malcolm malcolm, how are u do/en
We need to knoooow.

SISTUH: yes. minister malcolm i have watched u

(malcolm's future wife)

have seen u & know u to be true
yes. minister malcolm i will be yo/wife
and live with u all our life.

BROTHA: we'll have children who will live

(muslim malcolm)

who'll have lives that are positive
we'll raise them with love & care
they will be black muslims & aware

CHORUS, 3 SISTUHS: shots, shots. cries in the day.
SHOTS, SHOTS, CRIES IN THE DAY

*(softly then builds up to be sung slowly & sadly to blue/
bird)*

shots. shots. cries in the day.
SHOTS, SHOTS, CRIES IN THE DAY
malcolm, malcolm who killed u?
malcolm, malcolm who killed u?
malcolm, malcolm who killed u?
weeeeeee have to know.

SISTUH: *(screams & cries over him)*
(malcolm's wife runs to malcolm as he falls.)

malcolm m m m m m m m m m M M M M
malcolm m m m m m m m m m M M M M
malcolm m m m m m m m m m M M M M

SISTUH: i told u i am wite/amurica & i kill

*(wite/amurica with am/flag & confederate flag prances
around pointing at malcolm.)*

even/blk/nigguhs who try to fulfill
their destiny. wite/amurica am I
& i will never, never, die.
look. look. nigguhs full of tears
don't they know one man can't change my years
of rule. for wite/amurica am I
& i will never, never die.

BROTHA: *(falls on the ground)*
(dyin/malcolm)

i have been shot. i shall soon die.
my death means we should unify
don't worship my death. i will be gone
u must move on and on and on.
for life is now. with one who leads
not in the past with me who bleeds
so move on. move on. rememMMMMBER me.
but move on till blk/people are free. free. free.
so i die. but hear my sound
u must not hate you must be bound
to nationalism. to freedom. to yo/blk/land
let us move together and expand.

(moves back to line slowly, holden chest)

CHORUS, 3 SISTUHS: wite/amurica regrets, malcolm/man
don't live here no mo.

(sung slowly to miss otis regrets or any ridiculous tune)

oh yeh. yeh.
don't live here no mo.
wite/amurica regrets, malcolm/man
oh yeh. yeh.
But we blk/people remember him
will *always* remember him
cuz for him we'll unite
cuz for him we will fight
and keep his memory alive
and keep his truth alive
but we won't worship the dead
but we won't worship the dead
cuz the dead cannot lead

cuz the dead cannot lead
but we'll remember him
but we'll remember him
CUZ:
malcolm/man don't live here no mo
malcolm/man don't live here no mo
but, he showed us the score
but, he showed us the score
& we'll make it for him
& we'll make it for him.

Uh, Uh; But How Do It Free Us?

(1974)

CHARACTERS:

GROUP I

(Brother is stretched out across the bed and sisters are seated on outer sides of bed. One sister is reading.)

MALIK: *twenty years old, dressed in traditional clothes*

WALEESHA: *twenty-one years old, pregnant, sitting on the left side of the bed*

NEFERTIA: *eighteen years old, in traditional dress, sitting on the right side of the bed, reading a book*

GROUP II

(Four brothers, one devil, sitting on five/white/rocking/horses. A sister/whore and white whore stand on either side with whips.)

SISTER WHORE: *about twenty-five years old in tight/mini dress/long knee boots, black stockings and an expensive red/colored wig on her head*

WHITE WHORE: *about twenty-four years old in purple/see-through shirt and bell bottom pants. Has on boots and blond hair*

THREE BROTHERS AND ONE WHITE MAN: *ranging in ages twenty-six and thirty-four, dressed in bell bottoms, cowboy hats, big ties and jewelry*

BROTHER MAN: *about thirty-eight years old, dressed in dashiki with tiki and African hat*

GROUP III

(A screen separates a sister and a devil/woman [white woman]. On the sister's side of the screen are African masks and she sits on an African stool; there are suitcases on the floor. A table with a phone. On the devil/woman's side is pop art, a table with phone and phonograph, and a butterfly chair, where she lounges. The brother sits on pillows in

the middle of the floor. In front of the pillows is a table with liquor.)

BROTHER: *about thirty-four years old, has on two/toned suit, one side is brown suede with a big yellow flower in the center. One side is an orange dashiki with a brown/embroidered map of Africa, wears a talisman, tight/brown/suede/pants and sandals, shades and a floppy/suede hat*

SISTER: *about thirty-two years old, big natural, dressed in long dress*

DEVIL/WOMAN: *about thirty-three years old, plain-looking, light brown hair, dressed simply but richly*

DANCERS: *(Two brothers and two sisters, stretched out on the floor observing the three groups)*

SETTING: *(The lights are low at the beginning, just light enough to see the arrangement of the ACTORS in the three groups. The DANCERS are stretched out in front of the group as if waiting. . . As each group speaks the light is directed on them and the DANCERS move conspicuously/inconspicuously in front of them and watch and listen. When the talking ceases the DANCERS begin their talking.)*

TIME: *(NOW)*

(The light moves to GROUP I.)

WALEESHA: Are you goin' out again tonight, Malik?

MALIK: Yeah. Got a lot of people to see tonight 'bout the play we doing; then we have a rehearsal. Why, what's the matter? *(Raises up from the bed and looks in her direction)*

WALEESHA: Oh. I just wondered if you were gonna be home or not. *(Stands up, stretches; we see she's about seven or eight months pregnant.)* I just thought you might want to go to a show or something. Felt like doin' something this evening. I guess I'll knit. *(Picks up her knitting and for a few minutes the quiet sound of needles pierces the ears.)* Are you going also, Nefertia?

NEFERTIA:	*(Looks up from her book)* Uh, huh. We're rehearsing again tonight. But the play is real badddd. And Malik is the best. He's beautiful, Waleesha. You should see how the others just stop when he's onstage and just listen to him. It's like the brother who wrote the play was writing it just for Malik.
MALIK:	*(Turns toward NEFERTIA)* Do you really think so? I mean, I don't really feel that I have the necessary fire or depth for the second act. I mean, I say the words, but they don't feel true inside. You know what I mean? It . . . sometimes I think an older dude should play the part.
NEFERTIA:	It sounds fine to me. You are just a perfectionist, Malik. Always pushing yourself. You are a brilliant man. The part is you.
MALIK:	*(Gets up and walks around the room and stops in front of a long/mirror, turns and swaggers slightly)* Do you really think so?
NEFERTIA:	Man. You simply too much in it. Don't you remember when they were giving out parts they kept looking at you. I knew then that it was going to be yours. Remember how you thought at first that they hadn't cast you for anything. I saw you get uptight when some of the better roles were given. I knew then. Mannnnnn, I knew then that the part was yours. That my Malik had gotten the best, the main part of the play and was gon' to tear it up, be mean. The meanest. *(Is laughing at the end)*
WALEESHA:	Are you in the play also, Nefertia? I mean, now that you are three months pregnant it might be too much for you. Goin' to school and all.
NEFERTIA:	Girl, no. I ain't tired at all. *(Stands up and walks across the room slowly)* And, no one knows I'm pregnant yet. I haven't told them a word. As long as I'm small they won't know and have to be concerned.
WALEESHA:	But, sister, you should tell everyone; after all, it is an occasion for rejoicing. Is it not so, my husband? *(MALIK is looking at himself in the mirror.)* Malik, I said is it not

so that Nefertia's pregnancy should be a time of re-joicing?

MALIK: *(Turns around)* Yeah, and she don't even look pregnant, does she? I remember when you were three months pregnant, Waleesha, you were bigggggg. The doctor had to put you on a diet at three months. *(Laughs)* Do you remember?

WALEESHA: *(Stops knitting)* Yes. I ate a lot during those early months. It was around the time that Nefertia first moved in with us. Remember? *(Begins knitting again, and the sound of the needles clicking is heavy.)*

MALIK: Yeah, I remember. Well, I'm gonna split now. *(Goes to closet and gets his jacket)*

NEFERTIA: Wait a minute. I'll get my coat, too.

MALIK: No. I have a couple of stops to make. I'll be moving too fast for you. You come on later to the theatre. I'll meet you there.

WALEESHA: Do you want somethin' to eat before you go?

MALIK: Naw, I'll be eating where I'm goin'. Hey, I need a couple of dollars. Nefertia, did your school check come?

NEFERTIA: Yes. But I didn't git a chance to cash it. And I have only two dollars.

MALIK: That'll do. *(Walks over and takes two dollars)* See y'all later. *(Exits)*

WALEESHA: Yes. I was huge, wasn't I, when I wuz three months. No, it was really four months? Don't youuuu remember, Nefertia?

NEFERTIA: Uh huh. *(Reading again)*

WALEESHA: Yes, he is right. I was really big. Don't you think so, Nefertia?

NEFERTIA: *(Without looking up)* Uh huh.

WALEESHA: *(Raises her voice slightly)* Say something besides uh huh. I'm just trying to have some kind of conversation.

NEFERTIA: (*Without looking up*) No, you ain't. You just trying to start an argument. You know it. I know it. We both know it. That's why I don't answer ya.

WALEESHA: An argument? An argument 'bout what, Nefertia? What do we have to argue about?

NEFERTIA: (*Finally looks up*) 'Bout me. That's what. 'Bout Malik and me. That's what. You mad cuz I'm the second wife. You still mad at me, sister, and you know it.

WALEESHA: Why should I be mad at you? Just tell me why, Nefertia. Malik brought you here—you were his choice. His decision. And since I love him. I have to abide by his choice, no matter how unwise it may be. (*Stands up*) I guess I'll fix something to eat now. (*Stretches*) Ah. This warrior is kicking me hard. He's gon' be bad cuz he's bad already. Ah. He's moving again. (*Puts hands on stomach*) You want to feel little Maliki, Nefertia? You want to hear him running around this house of mine, playing his warrior games?

NEFERTIA: What I want to feel yo/stomach for? No. I got to finish this reading for tomorrow's class.

WALEESHA: (*Gets a can of beans and begins to open it. Begins to speak softly*) One thing's for sure, though. When I have my warrior the burden will be on you. Oh, yes. When I have my sweet Maliki, you'll be big and fat like me and you (*great laughs*) will have a longggggg nine months. Just you wait, just you wait. . .

NEFERTIA: You a bitch, you know, Waleesha. You and yo quiet/sneaky ways. How you know fo sure you gon' have a male/child? And what if it's a girl? Huh? What if it's a girl/child? And so what if you do have a male/child? I can have one too. Or even if I have a girl, Malik will love her just like he loves me now. Just like he loved me befo I came here to this house. He used to tell me about you. You and yo/knitting and going to the movies. And hardly ever interested in him, he said. He said you never saw him, never. He said you never read anything, not even a newspaper. We love each other becuz we have everything in common. Theatre, school, poetry. Ours is not just physical love, he says. It's mental, too. So it's you who don't really stand a chance here. I might have been chosen second, but he told me I saved him from you and yo/non/interest in anything. (*During the above, WALEESHA has warmed the beans and is making a salad. NEFERTIA moves over to her, still talking.*) Yes, Waleesha, I saved him from the boredom that is you. You dig? I am the second choice, but first in his heart. You dig it, sistuh?

WALEESHA: (*Sits down and begins to eat, and just before eating, looks up and slowly smiles*) Just you wait and see, sister. Just you wait and see. . .

(*Light fades and moves to DANCERS. One MALE DANCER stays stretched out watching. Moving to see better.*)

DANCERS: (*MALE DANCER walks across stage. Two SISTER DANCERS sitting down on imaginary chairs, one knitting the other reading. When he passes the knitting sister, he beckons to her and she gets up and follows him, knitting. Then, looking at him, knitting. MALE DANCER passes the SECOND SISTER reading.*

Stops. Turns around, escorts the first KNITTING SISTER back to other side of stage, constantly straining his neck to see OTHER SISTER. He turns the KNITTING SISTER around, back to him and audience. She stands mutely, knitting. MALE DANCER turns, jumps up and down joyously, walks, stops. Look in make-believe mirror. Flexes left leg, then the right leg. Combs his natural. Turns quickly around to look at the KNITTING SISTER. He sits down next to READING SISTER. Begins to read with her. Starts to rap. She looks up. Listens. He raps more. And still rapping, he removes her book. Touches her body, still rapping. Holds her as they dance a love dance. When she becomes mesmerized he takes her and puts her next to the KNITTING SISTER. He lines them up behind him and begins to walk around the stage, stopping at a mirror to preen. He returns to get the other two SISTERS, the KNITTING SISTER behind him and the READING SISTER behind the KNITTING SISTER. The READING SISTER keeps trying to move in front of the KNITTING SISTER but she is blocked each time. And the MALE DANCER never looks around. As the MALE DANCER walks, he keeps turning his head as he sees some other sisters, beckons, like as to "I'll see you later" look, spruces up. Stops at mirror again and does a preening dance. The second MALE DANCER on the floor laughs, rolls over the floor and laughs. Laughs. Laughs.)

(Light moves to GROUP II. All men riding their horses)

FIRST BROTHER: This horse is good.

SECOND BROTHER: The best ever.

THIRD BROTHER: Giddap, you goddamn horse. Faster. You too slow today. Gots to ride my horse a little higher today. Gots to go to the moooonnn. Soooonnnn. Boommmm. Boommmm. *(Laughs)*

WHITE DUDE: It's good being out that joint. It's gooood being free again. After two years. It's good being out. Ain't it, men?

BROTHER MAN: Yeah, mannnn. That place was a M.F. Eight years there. Amid everything. But I'm out now. And the first thing I said I wuz gon' do wuz to get the biggest fix in the world. It wuz gon' be so big that I would be the world. You diggit. I would be the world. Cuz, man, I got the biggest hustle in the whole wide world today. I found blackness in the joint, you dig, and I wrote a book and everything I write is licked up by everyone. The Blk/ prison/writer is a hero. All thanks is due to Malcolm/ man, Eldridge/man for making this all so simple. Man, I got it made after all these thirty-eight years of little hustles, little busts. I got it made. All praises is due to Blackness.

FIRST BROTHER: Hey, you Black/bitch. Git over here and do yo/job. What you gittin' paid for? You broken down whore. Git over here and pree-form. Right now. You ain't paid to stand around.

SECOND BROTHER: Yeah, make it over here, tootie suitie or we'll remove y'all.

Cuz we some bad ones right here. We the new breed, ain't we, man. *(This section is spoken fast. A climax of sorts. At the conclusion they return to their pleasant light/ high.)*

THIRD BROTHER: The new black man raging in the land. We the orga-nized/gangster Blk/man. We mean. We do what's to be done. We dealing. We the new Blk/mafia. We dealing.

FIRST BROTHER: Dealing? Man, do we deal. Look around ya and you see us. Dealing from city to city. Making money, bread. Controlling an entire Blk/community.

SECOND BROTHER: Yeah. We keep coming up four aces and the only thing beat four aces is a flush.

THIRD BROTHER: And if that shows, y'all knows toilets is for flushes! *(Laughs)*

FIRST BROTHER: We badddddd.

SECOND BROTHER: BadddddddER than bad.

THIRD BROTHER: Baddddder than a dude's bad breath.

FIRST BROTHER: We meannnnn.

SECOND BROTHER: Meaner than MEANNN.

THIRD BROTHER: Meaner than a dude whose corn you done stepped on.

FIRST BROTHER: We Blk/mafia/men.

SECOND BROTHER: Blk/on/Blk/mafia men

THIRD BROTHER: Blacker than Blk/mafia/men. Bother us and you'll see!

WHITE MAN: Come here, you. *(Beckons to WHITE WHORE)* Come here now. I want you to beat me again while I'm riding.

WHITE WHORE: No. I ain't coming this time. The last time you hurt me. You paying me to beat you. O.K. That's it. Nothing else. I won't do anything else. *(Turns to BROTHER MAN)* You said only the beating, nothing more, since y'all already had your lady. *(Points to horse)* You promised. The last time he was awful. What's wrong with him? Do he hate women or something?

WHITE MAN:	What you calling me, whore? You trying to call me something, you think something wrong with me? I got my stable together already. Out one week and I got three bitches breathing their desire over me already. They humpin' for me. Bring me all their money. They can do more than you can anyday, you anemic-looking witch.
BROTHER MAN:	(*Laughs softly*) Take it slow man. She just a little scared of you. You did take her through some deep changes. We had to pull you off her. Now, didn't we?
WHITE MAN:	She weak. She weak like all women. Don't need them, though. Got my girl. Cumon girl. Let's go. Let's you and me git a thing going. I want to feel you in my guts. Warming my insides. Making me feel good. Warm. Secure. Manly. Gots to git that again. C'mon over here, you purple bitch. Help me to come. Hit me, hurt me. Turn me inside out with pain. C'mon you dead-lookin' whore.
	(*WHITE WHORE moves over slowly. Begins to beat him softly. He screams. Harder. Beats him harder. And on the last hit, he grabs the whip and pulls her toward him. She screams. WHITE MAN gets off the horse. His movement is like a slow memory of death.*) What you doin' beating me, Momma? I didn't do anything. Really, I didn't say no dirty/bad/words. Momma. Please don't beat me. Please pull up my pants, Momma. You get so carried away you hit me all over.
WHITE WHORE:	There he goes again. Git him away from me. He's crazy.
BLACK WHORE:	Help her, you dudes. He crazier than you think. He gon' kill her. (*Moves to help and is blocked by BROTHER MAN*)
WHITE WHORE:	Help me. Don't let him hit me again. (*Tries to run away but is caught in the WHITE DUDE's massive arms*) I didn't mean to hit you. Please excuse me. Let me go now. I really have to go. Don't hit me again.
WHITE MAN:	(*Oblivious to all that has happened*) Momma. Why you always hitting me. I am good. I ain't gon' turn out bad.

There ain't no evil spirits inside me. Momma, don't hit me. I'm just seven years old. I wasn't doing nothing. Dottie and I were just playing house. OWWWW. Momma, I'm bleeding. Don't hit me so hard. I'll never play house again. Help me. Somebody help me. Daddy, come back and help me. Help me. *(Sobs)*

WHITE WHORE: *(Is on her knees now and her cries mingle with the WHITE MAN's cries.)* Help me. *(Sobs)*

BROTHER MAN: *(Still on horse)* They a sorry sight, you know.

FIRST BROTHER: Why you always letting him hang around here, man?

SECOND BROTHER: Yeah. It's one thing to do the biz—another to socialize with the dude. I mean, brother/man, he be weird.

THIRD BROTHER: You know when we wuz in the joint they caught him being somebody's "kid"—so what good is he anyway.

BROTHER MAN: I don't know. Perhaps you right. He's always hanging around. I guess I feel sorry for him in a way. I owe him something. When I first got out the joint, he saw me through till I could move around—get my thing straight. Look at the po/sorry/bastard. With a momma complex or something. Guess I should stop this madness. *(Turns and looks at BLACK WHORE)* What you think over there, Blk/whore? Should I stop it now? *(Moves over and puts WHITE DUDE back on horse. Talking softly to WHITE DUDE. Hands whip to WHITE WHORE. WHITE WHORE slides on away to the THIRD BLACK DUDE who helps her.)*

BLACK WHORE: Y'all some crazy dudes, but ya paying me so that's all I'm gon' say.

BROTHER MAN: *(Moving toward BLACK WHORE)* What's yo name, girl?

BLACK WHORE: Ain't got no name. Lost my name when I was eleven years old. I became just a body then so I forgot my name. Don't nobody want to know a Black woman's name anyway. You gon' take me home with ya to keep? Put me in your pocket to hold/touch when you need some warmth? No? Well, since you ain't, then there ain't no reason to tell ya my name. All ya need to know is on my face and body. If you can read a map you can read me.

BROTHER MAN: Yeah. Well, it's well traveled. But don't get smart with us. You are what you are cuz you wants to be. Don't go telling us nothing 'bout some dude turning you on when you was young. Every whore in the world says the same thing. Can't no dude in the world make you want to turn a trick less you inclined to do so. But y'all always blaming us Blk/men for your whoring, whore. You a whore cuz you wants to be, now ain't that so?

BLACK WHORE: Uh huh.

FIRST BROTHER: Is that all you gots to say is uh huh?

BLACK WHORE: Uh huh. Amen. And yassuh, boss.

SECOND BROTHER: You a smart whore ain't ya?

THIRD BROTHER: (Still helping the WHITE WHORE) Too smart, if you ask me. Never could stand no smart Black women anyhow. Always opening they mouths.

BROTHER MAN: Come over here, Black Whore.

BLACK WHORE: Yeah. I'm coming. I'm coming to receive my payment as usual on time, on schedule. For showing you just a little of yourselves whenever you see me.

BROTHER MAN: Get down on all fours.

BLACK WHORE: Yassuh, boss.

FIRST BROTHER: Man. Let me get down from my horse and git her.

BROTHER MAN: No, she's mine. (Puts a collar on her neck and climbs on her back and begins to ride her as he was riding the wooden horses) What kind of a day is it today, Black Whore?

BLACK WHORE: How in the hell I'm spoze to know, man, since I've been in here with ya crazy dudes all day.

BROTHER MAN: (Pulls collar hard till BLACK WHORE cries out) Would you say the sun is shining?

BLACK WHORE: (Quickly, sensing danger) Yes, it is. The sun is shining.

BROTHER MAN: How is that so when I wore my raincoat in here today? Are you suggesting I'm crazy or something for wearing my raincoat, Black Whore? You think you know better than me, Black/woman/whore?

BLACK WHORE: I mean the sun was shining for a while but it started to rain. Now it's raining. It's steady raining outside.

BROTHER MAN: *(Smiles)* Is it still raining, Black Whore?

BLACK WHORE: Yessir. Mr. Brother Man. It's raining.

BROTHER MAN: Still raining? I can't believe that for this time of year. Take me over to the window so I can see if it's raining or not. Giddap now, blk/horse. Giddap. I know you ain't gon' take me higher cuz only the white horse can do that. Hey, stop here for a minute. Them dudes got some coke that look goooood. Gots to git some of that now. *(BLACK WHORE takes him slowly over to the three BLACK DUDES and the WHITE DUDE.)* Is it any good?

FIRST BROTHER: I'm ten feet tall and gittin' taller.

SECOND BROTHER: I am god. I am god. I am god.

THIRD BROTHER: Get me a woman. No, get me five women. I need five women to satisfy what I see in my mind. Send out for some more women. Ya hear me?

WHITE DUDE: I rule the universe. I am the universe. The universe revolves around me. I am the universe. I am a man. A man. A man. Can't no one surpass me. I am a man. The man. A man. The man.

BROTHER MAN: This stuff must be good. Give me some. Now *(Smiles a long smile)* here's some for you, Black Whore. I know you just itching for some. Here, have some of mine.

BLACK WHORE: *(Reaches for it hesitantly, then takes it greedily. Becomes more relaxed)* Thank you, Brother Man.

BROTHER MAN: Think nothing of it, Black whore. Now, let us continue our trip toward weatherland. *(Laughs)* Whew! That stuff is baddddd. Whoa. Blk/whore. *(Turns)* Man, is that any of our stuff? It is. That too good for the niggers outside. They don't need that stuff at all. Whew! That's goooood, lady. Awright. Giddap, Black Whore. We got a destiny with the weather.

BLACK WHORE: *(Softly, mumblingly)* Our destiny is over, my man. We're yesterday.

BROTHER MAN: *(Stops the BLACK WHORE)* Whoa! What you say, whore? What you mumbling; ain't you satisfied? Didn't I just give ya some coke? Now, didn't I? I mean, ain't ya satisfied? Are you just the typical Black/woman? Always complaining never satisfied. Always bitching about something. What's wrong, you want some more coke, don't ya? Yeah, that's it. C'mon. Ima gonna see to it that you personally get more coke. *(Turns)* Hey you dudes, c'mon off and get some more coke for the lady here. I mean, let's share it with this no-name whore here. Why she could be your sister. Maybe somebody's momma? Hey, whore, is you somebody's momma? Huh? You somebody's momma? You got a kid? *(Pulls collar tightly)* Answer me, bitch. I'm talking to you. The new Blk/man in America. The successful Blk/man in America. Answer me now.

BLACK WHORE: Yes. I have a kid.

BROTHER MAN: You a mother. It figures, though. You all have one kid or something living with some old woman or something and you visit there on holidays and bring presents and hugs and kisses and promises of an earlier visit, right?

BLACK WHORE: That's right.

FIRST BROTHER: Hey, how you know that, man? That sounds like my ole lady. I didn't know what she was 'till someone told me 'bout her. I always thought she was a teacher or something.

SECOND BROTHER: She was a teacher all right, man. She was steady teaching dudes all they needed to know to git by. She still humping, man?

FIRST BROTHER: Man, she died last year. O.D. When I got in the bizness, I had one of my boys run her some good stuff. Guess it was too much for her. They found her in her room, sleeping like a baby. In fact, when I saw her laid out she looked like I remembered her to be when I was little and thought she was a queen. A beautiful queen.

BROTHER MAN: They saying today that Blk/women are queens. Did y'all know that? Have you heard any of that stuff, Blk/whore?

BLACK WHORE: Yeah. Some of the younger dudes talk to me sometimes. Say I should stop this stuff. They say I'm a queen, the mother of the universe. A beautiful Blk/woman/queen.

BROTHER MAN: Do you believe it?

BLACK WHORE: No. I know I ain't no queen. Look at me. I'm a whore. I know it. It just that they young. They see Blk/women differently. They say I'm not responsible for what I am. They say. . . . (Stops)

BROTHER MAN: Don't stop. Continue on.

BLACK WHORE: Aww, it ain't nothing but a lot of talk.

BROTHER MAN: Some call it rhetoric. Go on, finish it. I want to hear who is responsible.

BLACK WHORE: They say—it ain't me saying it, now, they say that we're the way we are because the men, the dudes, the brothers our age couldn't see us as anything else except whores, suz they couldn't see themselves as anything else except pimps or numbers runners or junkies or pushers, or even. . . . (Stops)

BROTHER MAN: Don't stop now. Hey, ya'll. C'mon over here, y'all are missing a education. Git your behinds over here and listen to our Blk/whore. She gon' rap on what's wrong with us all. Continue now. Or even—

BLACK WHORE: Awwww, man. It ain't me. I'm just repeating what they done told me. It ain't my words.

BROTHER MAN: Continue, I said.

BLACK WHORE: Or even the Blk/gangsters who go round thinking they baddddd. All they doing is repeating themselves out loud. Cuz they still hurting, killing, selling dope to our people, and they don't know that instead of having a little bit of the planet, that the planet earth is ours. All ours just waiting to be taken over.

BROTHER MAN: You believe that, girl?

BLACK WHORE: No. Course not. Just some young punks rapping hard.

BROTHER MAN: Would you like to believe it, girl? I mean, would you like to be a queen of the universe, c'mon. Get up off ya knees. Ya, a queen. Hey, White Whore, bring the fur coat out the closet and some makeup. Hurry up. We got a queen here. Waiting to be fixed up. *(Everyone moves around the BLACK WHORE, fixing her up till they step back and see her dressed up.)* Everyone bow. No. Altogether. On the count of three. Everyone bow and say yo/majesty. One, two, three, yo/majesty. C'mon. Louder than that. One, two, three, yo/majesty. Yeah. That's better now, yo/majesty. Walk around and view your subjects. Walk around and see what your kingdom's about. Go ahead, now, we ain't gon' hurt you any, go on now.

(The BLACK WHORE begins to walk shakily. She's obviously scared. But as she walks, she relaxes, and as she passes by the second time, her face changes and her body seems taller. She looks queenly, like a latter day Lady Day looked on TV, nervous and unsure but queenly.)

WHITE DUDE: Stop it. What is this sheeeeet? Who she think she is anyway? If anyone's gon' be queen of the universe around here, it's gon' be me. *(Goes to closet, puts on coat, high heel shoes, wig, earrings. Turns around slowly and walks sensuously toward the group)* Here now. Look at me. I'm your queen of the universe. *(Begins to switch all around the room. The DUDES begin to laugh. Loudly clap.)* See, I'm the real queen. I am the universe. And I'm a queen, too. I'm the queen of the universe. Look at me everybody. Don't look at her. She's black. I'm white. The rightful queen. Look at me everybody. Your queen for today, for tomorrow, forever. The only queen for America. You get your queen some coke right now. *(WHITE WHORE brings some coke from one of the DUDES.)*

And don't you forget that I'm the queen, you hear? Get back over there, you purple witch you. *(Takes his coke)*

BROTHER MAN: All right, we have two contestants for the prize of "queen of the universe." Here they are, America. Look at them. Hear ye, hear ye. All you dudes, c'mon over here. You, too, White Whore. We're having a contest to find out which one is the true queen of the universe. The decision of us the judges will be final. All right, the contest begins. Begin your walk, all you would-be queens.

(The two queens walk around the room. As they move, the BLACK WHORE becomes more regal and silent and the switching sounds and sighs of the WHITE DUDE become shrill. As they make a final turn, the WHITE DUDE moves in front of the BLACK WHORE and blocks her path. She moves aside and he moves in front of her. She moves aside and he moves in front of her again. She moves aside and he moves in front of her and as she moves he punches her in the stomach and face. She falls to the floor. And the WHITE/ DUDE/QUEEN continues his walk and each time he passes the BLK/WHORE he kicks her.)

WHITE DUDE: It is obvious that I'm the queen. Is that right?

BROTHER MAN: Without a doubt. You've proved the point, man. The only queens in the world are white. And probably men. It's a good lesson for sorry whores who listen to young dudes rapping 'bout nothing, cuz me and my men are the time. It's the 1970s, and don't ya forget it. The decade of the hustles. The hustlers. The decade of easy/good/long/bread if you willing to take chances. We know who we are. We take off banks now. Run the whole dope operation in the Black communities. We run it and we run it well. *(Turns to the THREE BROTHERS)* Where y'all going tomorrow?

FIRST BROTHER: Detroit, man. A big shipment tomorrow.

SECOND BROTHER: Chicago. Got a meeting going with some Black cops who'll make sure things stay cool.

THIRD BROTHER: Louisville. Having a little trouble with one of the lieutenants there. Nothing serious. If need be, he goes.

BROTHER MAN:

C'mon. Let's take off one more time before we split. Queens. Not in my time. Get off the floor, Blk/Whore. C'mon, do yo/preordained/work.

(Men get on their horses and wait. The WHORES come over and begin to beat/hit them with a rhythm and they ride their horses. Quietly staring out at the audience, each one involved with his own orgiastic dreams. Light moves to the DANCERS.)

DANCERS:

(MALE DANCER is obviously a LITTLE BOY. Looks lost. Alone. Moving around stage. Looks up and sees a "MAMMA" FEMALE DANCER. Runs toward her but she knocks him down. He runs toward her again, but she knocks him down. He runs toward her again, but she knocks him down. Keeps going, begins to play with other FEMALE DANCER. She's a LITTLE GIRL. Playing house—mama and daddy. She hugs him. He hugs her. The MAMMA FEMALE walks past. Pulls them apart. Begins thrashing, killing dance, and leaves the YOUNG BOY sitting alone. Within himself. And as he sits, he grows older. Becomes a MAN. And a "LITTLE GIRL" female dancer, about eleven years old, passes by him and he watches her. Sees she is being stalked by an OLDER MALE DANCER. He watches, fascinated by it all. The two DANCERS [LITTLE GIRL/OLDER MAN] return now together. She is following. The OLDER MALE DANCER comes over to MALE DANCER [sitting down] and offers him the YOUNG GIRL. The three DANCERS dance a new/orgiastic/blue-bird-blue-bird through my window dance and the LITTLE GIRL DANCER goes mad and becomes a woman and we'll never know the exact moment her childhood ends. The three DANCERS move down the street and the two MALE DANCERS turn the YOUNG CHILD WOMAN DANCER over to another FEMALE DANCER who begins to console her caressingly. The two MALE dancers move off together and shyly begin to touch each other. Discordant music is heard!)

(Light fades and moves to GROUP III. The BROTHER slowly moves from the pillows. He has a disturbed look on his face. He mixes himself a long drink, turns around and looks at the two WOMEN in each separate room. They are both reading. He shakes his head, turns, and finishes his drink. He picks up

a red/blk/green pillow and goes to the SISTER side first, and he must stand or sit always with the dashiki side showing and never show the other side while visiting the SISTER.)

SISTER: *(Walks to BROTHER)* Well, I'm here. I finally made it. Three thousand miles from cold NYC to you and San Francisco.

BROTHER: Uh huh. I thought once that you wouldn't but you did. You a strong sister.

SISTER: I have to be, man. You a strong brother, and you ain't got no time for nobody who's weak.

BROTHER: Uh huh.

SISTER: What wrong, honey? You seem distant. Is something wrong?

BROTHER: No. Well, not wrong, but I have to go out tonight. To see this dude about something. Ain't sure I'm gon' git back tonight. And this yo/second night in town. Just wanted to be with you every night since you've finally come to me.

SISTER: Business is business, my man. I still have a lot of un-packing to do. The movement comes before you and me, love/making and all. When you have to TCB, you have to. *(She moves away from him and begins to busy herself.)* Now you git stepping and if you git a chance, call me. I'll be okay. Man, don't look so sad. We've got a whole lifetime of touching, loving, ahead of us.

BROTHER: I just want you to know, lady. You'll never regret coming out here to me. I'll take good care of you. Your family still mad about your coming?

SISTER: And how. They said you just can't pick up and go three thousand miles to a man you've only known six months. My father said, he needs to shave off that big beard of his. He looks like Castro. And what does he do? When I told them, you were in school getting your master's, they wanted to know then how would you support me. I told them that the new/Blk/woman didn't worry about a man taking care of her. She and her man work together. If he had no job, she worked and let him do the work of organizing the people. Since the money came from the oppressor, it didn't matter who made it. My mother stared at me in disbelief. Well, girl, she said, the new/Blk/woman, as you call her, is a first-class fool and had better git that part 'bout support straight right away cuz any Blk/man who don't think he has to support you will eventually begin to think you a fool, too, for letting him get away with it.

You gon' end up in a heap of trouble. And it went on and on like that every day till I left. My mother finally told me that it would have been better if I hadn't read all those books. She finally hugged me and said if I got into trouble to call her right away cuz wuzn't no—what's that he calls himself?—I said, revolutionary Black man—well, wasn't no revolutionary Black man gon' hurt her one and only daughter with no foreign talk. She said we Blk/women been fighting a long time just to get Blk/men to take care of us now you and yo/kind gon' to take us back. Girl, I think we older women needs to talk to y'all 'bout something called common sense. Then we hugged again and that's all. *(Goes to BROTHER and hugs him and becomes playful)* Then I jumped on a plane, no wagon train for this sister, and California here I wuz. And you were at the airport with a rose, one lone red rose. And I thought, man, that's beautiful. I'm going to press that rose in the first book you sent me. Do you remember?

BROTHER: Yeah. It was Fanon's *Studies in a Dying Colonialism,* wasn't it?

SISTER: Uh huh.

BROTHER: Well, baby. I gots to split, but bizness is calling me tonight. I'll try to call you. If I don't, I'll send some sisters to bring you out to the school tomorrow. All right? *(Kisses her and picks up the red/blk/green pillow and leaves)*

(SISTER, for a moment she stands as if waiting, then begins quick movements. Goes over to one of the suitcases and be-

gins to unpack. BROTHER returns to the middle of stage and puts the red/blk/green pillow down. Crosses to table, pours himself another drink, turns, peers to the right, picks up a red velvet pillow and enters the WHITE WOMAN's apartment.)

BROTHER: Greetings from afar. Your boy/wonder has returned.

WHITE WOMAN: How was your trip down the peninsula?

BROTHER: Not bad. We'll talk about that later, but now some food and drink for one who has traveled so far to partake of your charms. *(Slightly drunk)*

WHITE WOMAN: *(Smiling, but serious)* Ah, my man, you are most definitely mad. And didn't you promise me that you would cut down on your drinking? You got blotto, no, now what is it you say. . . ?

BROTHER: Wasted, my love.

WHITE WOMAN: Yes. You got wasted night before last. I had to put you to bed. That's no good. How are we going to change this diseased world if you're drunk?

BROTHER: I know. You know it's just these recent happenings. Like you know, it's hard to leave you sometimes, and you know I'll have my new family starting next week. It's just so hard. You see, she doesn't know anything about you. She could never understand you and me and her and me at the same time, you being white and all.

WHITE WOMAN: Now, my man, it's your decision to make. *(Gets up and fixes two drinks)* If it's too much we can stop seeing each other. I'm not here to destroy you or make you feel guilty. I love you, my man, and whatever decision you make I'll abide by. *(Hands drink to BROTHER)* But since you're moving up in the movement out here, you do need a Blk/woman image. She's cute looking. Small. Compact, with a good/growing/awareness of what's to be done. You made a good choice, and she obviously adores you. I saw how she was watching you in New York. You are her life. So she'll be dedicated to you and you need a Blk/woman who will dedicate her life to you, for you are becoming a very important man out here. But people are noticing that you don't have a Blk/ woman.

BROTHER: You're a rare woman, you know. Not many women would share their man the way you do. You know, I wuz coming here tonight to say that we had to stop seeing each other. That since she's coming next week, it wouldn't be fair to both of you, that you both would be cheated in some way. But you've made it so simple. Since we understand, we can keep this just between us. And she'll never know. *(Hands empty glass to WHITE WOMAN)* How's about another one of those goodie good drinks you fix for you VIP's huh? Then some good dinner for a hard-working revolutionary. *(Brother sits on pillow.)*

WHITE WOMAN: *(Moves over to BROTHER and sits down next to him)* After we eat, could we go to the club and see John Handy? I haven't seen him since your birthday. Let's go out tonight. Make it a grand celebration since my wandering warrior has returned from the peninsular wars.

BROTHER: Girl, I'm tired. Just wants to sleep for a coupla days. *(Turns and sees her face)* But. . . all right. I tell ya not for long. Just for one set. Now go fix my food. RAT NOW! Y'all hear? This nigger is ready to grease out loud.

(WHITE WOMAN gets up and moves behind the screen. The BROTHER goes over to phone and dials a number. We see the SISTER stretched out on the floor and she picks up the phone on the first ring.)

How you doing, baby? Were you sleeping?

SISTER: No. Just dreaming, 'bout you and me, and us, 'bout our yet unborn children waiting for us. To be born. Just thinking good things 'bout us, man. 'Bout what will be cuz we, this new Blk/man Blk/woman will finally put to rest the thoughts that we can't/don't git along. It wuz good news, man, just like you good news for me.

BROTHER: Yeah. I feel the same way 'bout you. You beautiful people, and I'm happy you here. We got a whole lot of work to do, and to do it with someone like you should be a gasssss. Look, baby, this meeting is taking longer than I thought. I won't be able to get back over to ya. I gots a lot of talking to do this night, so you close yo/ eyes and continue to dream 'bout me. Us. Our future, just continue to dream 'bout us. Don't let nothing interfere with that. Yo/dreams of us. Me and you. As long as we're together in yo/dreams we will BE. Remember that, baby. Just remember that. Don't you ever forget that you my woman. My Black woman. The woman I'ma gonna show to the world. My choice for the world to see.

SISTER: I love you, man. I love only you. Been waiting for you for a long time, and now that we together, time had better git stepping cuz it's you and me now and nothing's gon' git in our way.

BROTHER: Git some sleep now, baby. I'll see you tomorrow. Later on.

(BROTHER hangs up and moves behind the screen. SISTER hangs up, gets up and happiness is on her face. She does a quick spin and lets out a loud laugh. Stretches out on floor and goes to sleep. At the same time you see the BROTHER and WHITE WOMAN dancing past. Talking. Laughing.)

WHITE WOMAN: And I thought you had forgotten my birthday.

BROTHER: (Smiles) I thought you thought that. I just didn't mention it to you because I wasn't sure if I would be able to buy you what I wanted to. I solved it all, however. I wrote a bad check that's so full of rubber it'll bounce from here to the Golden Gate Bridge.

WHITE WOMAN: (Laughs) You're incorrigible. (Moves away from him and hands him a letter) Here you are. On time as usual, my man. Now, don't you do that again.

BROTHER: (Doesn't raise his hand to accept the letter. Turns away and flops down in the chair) I ain't gon' take no more of yo/ money, girl. I'll/we'll, she and I will have to make it on her check and the school check. It was all right befo but no mo. Not now. It wouldn't seem right.

WHITE WOMAN: Ahhhhh, my man. That's what I love about you. Your values. You know you two can't get along on the money you're both making, that part-time teaching job she has can't/won't really help. I mean the money is rightfully yours. I told you that a long time ago, it's the money that my father got by underpaying Black people for years. It's rightfully yours. It should go to a Black man twisting and turning to be someone. Twisting and turning to survive it all. *(Moves to table and puts the check down. Pours two drinks)* It's really amusing. The estate sends me all this money and I give it to you and you travel around. Talk. Organize. Get people to change the world so no more men like my father will exist. If my mother only knew, she would have one very real attack instead of one of her many fake ones. *(Hands BROTHER a drink)*

BROTHER: Yeah. It just seems weird taking care of her with your checks.

WHITE WOMAN: But, baby, she deserves it too. After all she's Black and she works hard, too. She's a sort of inspiration to Black women. *(Taking a sip)*

BROTHER: Don't you. . . well, don't you envy her or hate her at all? She comes down hard on white women, you know.

WHITE WOMAN: Yes, she does. But I understand her bitterness, loneliness. She's had a very hard life. Not many people would have survived it. No. I don't hate her. After all, she says a lot of truth. *(Crosses over and sits down in front of BROTHER)* A lot of white women do love Blk/men. She feels threatened by this. *(Kisses him, then takes down her hair. Lets it flow on him, his face, as he stretches out and pulls her on top of him.)*

BROTHER: I don't know what I'd do without you, baby. You good to me.

WHITE WOMAN: Don't try to. Everything is as it should be. I can share you any time as long as you always turn up here. Drunk or sober. You hear? *(Holds his head as she talks)* You are mine, my man. I found life, a reason for living, when I found you. I live from the light you bring me. When you stand up to talk and I hear you telling your brothers and sisters what we've discussed, I feel all warm inside. I see me up there on stage, and it's so good.

BROTHER: Come here, you, and say it's so goooood again.

WHITE WOMAN: *(Moves on him and covers his face with her hair)* It's so gooooooood, my man.

(Light moves to the BLACK WOMAN's side, she's on the floor, exercising. Her rhythm on the floor corresponds to the sounds coming from the WHITE WOMAN'S side. When she's finished, she relaxes at the same time the WHITE WOMAN and BLACK MAN separate and rest alongside each other. BLACK WOMAN stands up and you see she's pregnant. Early stages of pregnancy. Holds up a beautiful long dress and puts it on a hanger. Turns when she hears the door open.)

SISTER: Hey. What's happening? Look at this dress. I made it this morning. *(Holds it up to her body)* How do you like it?

BROTHER: You'll be tough, baby. Are you speaking tonight?

SISTER: Yes, at the cultural center. It should be a good crowd. Imagine having five crazy poets onstage together. The Black Experience indeed! It's gon' be smoking tonight. I just did a new poem tonight for the sisters at San Francisco State. It's called "To All Sisters." Listen to it.

> what a white woman got
>> cept her white pussy
>>> always sucking after blk/ness
> what a white woman got
>> cept her straight hair
>>> covering up her fucked up mind
> what a white woman got
>> cept her faggoty white man
>>> who goes to sleep on her
>>>> without
>>>>> coming

what a white woman got
cept money trying to buy up
a blk/man?
yeah.
what a white woman got?

(As the SISTER reads the poem, the BROTHER's face and body tense. When she finishes, he sits down.)

BROTHER: You coming down kinda hard, ain't you, baby?

SISTER: Hard. Can't nobody be too hard on the devil/woman. She's the same as the devil/man, ain't she? One of the sisters came into my office today saying her old man has one. He said that it was a political move. So she asked him what's political about a devil/woman since she thought we were talking about all white people, not just white men. She said he looked at her and said you don't know what's happening. That the only way he as a Black man could maneuver would be to have a well/to/do/white chick in his corner. Man, she's all torn up so when I come home I wrote this poem. That's why it's got to be baddddddd—baddddddddder than bad so we can put that white woman in her proper perspective, you dig? Tell me, man what's happening with Greg, huh? Frances is a beautiful sister. Loyal, hard working. What is on his mind, man?

BROTHER: *(Looks up. Worried)* How in the hell should I know? I don't know what's on that nigger's mind. It's his business, not ours. *(Stands up)* Look, baby. I got a whole lot on my mind. Johnny and I are leaving tomorrow night for Mexico to hook up with some revolutionaries down there, so I ain't got no time to figure out the workings of some dude's mind.

SISTER: Oh, I'm sorry, man, but you know what's happening here. It was just on my mind, and I had to spit it out. Had to. Sometimes this is just so unreal. I mean, sisters really working hard at being true Black women. Really hard. And then some dude takes them out, so far out to lunch that they might never come back. Couldn't you speak to him, mannn?

BROTHER: *(Impatient)* Yeah. When I come back, I'll talk to him, O.K.? Now miss do-good lady, would you please pack me a bag before you go out?

SISTER: *(A worried look)* You not coming with me tonight? Oh no. But you promised, mannnnnnnn. Our last night together, you promised it would be our night. You'll be gone a whole week.

BROTHER: Too tired, baby. Had meetings all day with the people here who are to hook us up in Mexico.

SISTER: *(Sulking)* I know, but you promised.

BROTHER: So what? What you sulking 'bout? So I Promised. I'm here, ain't I? I ain't goin' no place tonight. When you come back, I'll be here waiting for you. I just don't feel like hearing no poets up on a stage talking bad. *(Smiles)* It's just hard for me, you know, to see you up there on stage gittin' all that applause. Makes me begin to wonder why you chose me. After all, I'm not real famous yet. I'm working on it. But you, everybody knows you so. . .

SISTER: Ah, man. I understand now. It's alright. Look, I'll leave as soon as I read. So I can come home to you, man, to one who has chosen me from afar. *(The bell rings.)* There they are. I'll run on downstairs. They'll bring me home. You get some rest, mannn, cuz when I come back. . . *(Smiles)*

BROTHER: Do it to them, baby. See you soon.

(BROTHER fixes drink and picks up the phone. He hesitates. A worried look on his face. Dials the phone. Phone rings. On the WHITE WOMAN's side the phone rings and rings and rings and she looks up and continues to read. BROTHER puts down the receiver and dials again. The phone rings and rings and the WHITE WOMAN gets up and fixes herself a drink. Puts some music on and picks up the phone and dials. BROTHER jumps for the phone.)

WHITE WOMAN: Greetings, my man. How are you? Thought I'd take a chance and call you there.

BROTHER:	Uh huh. Where are you? I've been trying to get you all night.
WHITE WOMAN:	Why, I'm home. I've been here all night. Thinking about you.
BROTHER:	I've been calling you all night. And the phone just rang and rang. Where you been?
WHITE WOMAN:	I told you. No place, just here. You must have dialed a wrong number.
BROTHER:	Bitch. What you take me for, a fool?
WHITE WOMAN:	*(Coldly)* Impregnating women is a criteria for revolution?
BROTHER:	You think Black babies ain't part of change?
WHITE WOMAN:	How are we going to have time for a baby? There's no place for children now. I thought you had better sense than that. There's too much work to be done to stop and have a baby. Too much hard work to be done. That baby will tie you down, my mannn. You been together six months, and she's pregnant already.
BROTHER:	Just leave her out of this. She's happy about the baby. Just leave her out of this. *(Coldly)* If you worried about supporting us all, just stop worrying. When I return from Mexico, I'm gon' git a part/time/job to tide us over. Don't you worry about us at all. Look. I better hang up. Got some packing to do tonight. I'll call you from Mexico. *(There's no answer.)* Are you there? Hey. What's wrong?
WHITE WOMEN:	I'm crying.
BROTHER:	Why? I've been away before.
WHITE WOMEN:	I'm crying because for the first time I was being a bitch. I was jealous of her. She's carrying your child inside her. She's tied to you forever. You can leave anytime you want to. You just need. . . want. . . me for my money. That's all you want me for is my money. *(Begins to scream. Cry)*

BROTHER: Stop that now. Get yourself together and stop! Hear me? Do you hear me? Answer me. Do you hear me? (WHITE WOMAN sits crying by the phone. Listens to him calling her. Lights a cigarette and listens. She stops crying and sits silently.) Answer me. Do you hear me? Are you all right? Speak to me. Answer me. Are you all right? Don't do anything silly now, you still got those sleeping tablets in your house? Answer me. Do you hear me? Do you still have those sleeping tablets in your house? Hey, answer me!

(BROTHER hangs up phone, takes a drink, walks back and forth. Drinking. Thinking. WHITE WOMAN takes a drink. Walks back and forth. Finally stretches out on the floor and waits. BROTHER leaves the SISTER's house and enters the WHITE WOMAN's house, sees her on the floor and tries to wake her up. She's motionless.)

Hey, lady. Wake up. Are you all right? Hey, lady. C'mon now. I'm sorry for making you cry. Did you take anything, huh? I'm sorry it took me so long to get here. Couldn't get a cab. I finally had to walk/run here. Are you all right, baby? My baby. (Puts her hand in his lap and kinda croons the words "my baby" over and over again like a chant) My baby. You gon' be all right. You not gon' leave me. Your mannn. We're together forever. I am committed to you, lady. Don't nobody mean to me what you meant to me. C'mon, baby, you gonna be all right. I'm yo/mannnn. Nothing can change that, you know. So what if she's having a baby. It's something she wanted. I guess it fulfills her as a Black woman, but it didn't bother you and me, baby. Not us. We were together before she came and we'll stay together. Why, lady, you've made me all that I am. I'm almost finished with school because of you. I can travel whenever I want to because of you. I dress well because of you. I never want for money because of you. I'm a man because you've allowed me to be a man. Say you all right, baby. (Moves her head back and forth) C'mon, baby, speak to me.

WHITE WOMAN: (Speaks dully) Where am I?

BROTHER:	Ah. Thank God, here with me. What did you take, lady?
WHITE WOMAN:	(Slowly) I took some sleeping tablets with a glass of scotch.
BROTHER:	Lady. What you do that for? You had no reason to do that. What would I do if something happened to you? How would I make it without you? I neeed you, lady. Don't scare me like that.
WHITE WOMAN:	(Slowly) I just felt so lonely. So all alone. And I thought, he'll leave me one day. (Tries to sit up and BROTHER helps her.) He'll leave me one day just with the memory of three years together. Just with the sound of my door opening and shutting. He'll leave me and I'll dry up without his light. Without his sun. And I didn't want to see that day, my mannn. Do you understand? Don't be mad with me. You called me a bitch and I knew you were mad at me and I am a bitch. . . .
BROTHER:	No, not you. You're my life. I was just mad at you because you weren't home on my last night.
WHITE WOMAN:	I was home, my love. I was just trying to make you jealous. Forgive me, my mannn. Forgive this foolish honky/woman. Devil/woman as yo/Black/woman calls me.
BROTHER:	Hush now. And don't call yo/self those names.
WHITE WOMAN:	But I am a honky. A devil. Am I not? Isn't she talking about me, mannnn?
BROTHER:	No, she ain't. Not about you. You exceptional, lady. There ain't nobody like you. You no honky, or devil or none of those names. You're my woman. You understand that? If she has to call names and identify whites by certain names that's her business. But you and I know it's not you she's talking about. You're the most humane person in the world.
WHITE WOMAN:	Ah, man. Say you love me.
BROTHER:	I love you.

WHITE WOMAN:	Say you're all mine.
BROTHER:	I'm all yours, all yours.
WHITE WOMAN:	And you'll need me always.
BROTHER:	I'll need you always.
WHITE WOMAN:	(Stretches back out and puts her head in his lap) Stay the night with me, man.
BROTHER:	I can't. I promised. . . .
WHITE WOMEN:	Say you'll stay the night with me until I go to sleep. Please. It's your last night. If you stay I'll be able to get myself straight. Please.
BROTHER:	All right, baby. Let me call home, O.K.?
	(WHITE WOMAN gets up. Slowly. And moves behind the screen. BROTHER goes to the phone and dials and the phone rings at the same time the BLACK WOMAN enters her apartment. She picks up the phone.) Hey. You just get in? How was the reading?
SISTER:	Oh, fine. Mannn. Where are you?
BROTHER:	I got a call from one of the organizers of the trip. Something came up, I can't talk about it on the phone. Look. I should be home soon. Would you start packing my clothes for me? I'll be there soon.
SISTER:	But—but—but—why?
BROTHER:	Now, no questions. Just do as you're told. And we'll talk when I get there. Later.
	(Hangs up the phone. SISTER stands with the phone in her hand. Finally hangs it up. Moves and takes three suitcases out and opens them and methodically begins to pack each one of them. Slowly. Crooning a low mournful song. Maybe "Sometimes I Feel Like a Motherless Child." BROTHER is fixing himself a drink when WHITE WOMAN comes from behind the screen. She has on a natural wig and long dress.)
WHITE WOMAN:	Well, how do I look?
BROTHER:	Fine. Just fine, lady. You lookin' good.

WHITE WOMAN: I wanted to surprise you. Do I have the natural look she's always talking about?

BROTHER: Yes, you do.

WHITE WOMAN: Come here, my man. *(BROTHER moves to her and kisses her.)* Who do you love?

BROTHER: You, lady.

WHITE WOMAN: And who am I?

BROTHER: My woman.

WHITE WOMAN: And thou should have no other woman besides me. For I am all that you need. I can be all that you want. *(Spins away from him)* I can be natural when you need naturalness. *(Takes off wig)* Or I can be me when you want me. I am all things for you. *(Moves back to him excitedly)*

I know, let's get married. Right here tonight. Let us marry one another to each other.

BROTHER: Aw, lady, I don't know, that sounds, well, I don't know.

WHITE WOMAN: What's wrong with vowing to each other to love eternally? You didn't mean what you said, evidently.

BROTHER: No. It just seems unnecessary. But if you want to, why not?

WHITE WOMAN: Good. You go over to that side and I'll walk from this side. We'll kneel together and say our vows.

BROTHER: What should I say?

WHITE WOMAN: Just say what I say. All right? *(Both move to a separate part of the room and walk toward each other. Meet. And kneel, facing the audience)* We have come to declare our love. This white woman and Black man. We have come to speak out loud our love so that the night will hear us and know. *(Turns to BROTHER)* I love you, Black man.

BROTHER: *(Turns to WHITE WOMAN)* I love you, White woman.

WHITE WOMAN: And the words are spoken. And what can take back the words which represent the feelings, time and place and the words will travel throughout the land and make this universe stop and listen because I have said I love you Black man and his reply was love. The words have been spoken. And we are. Now. We have spoken in the night but the morning light will know. For the night and the morning are one. As we are one and our love shall be eternal.

BROTHER: And our love shall be eternal.

WHITE WOMAN: For you are the light. The energy. The sun. And I receive your light and live. And grow stronger each day. For you are my light, otherwise, I shall dwell in darkness. And together we are the universe. Light and darkness, strength and weakness. One and two. *(Turns to BROTHER)* Say we are one.

BROTHER: We are one.

WHITE WOMAN: You are the light and I am your darkness.

BROTHER: I am yo/light and you are my darkness.

WHITE WOMAN: We need each other to be.

BROTHER: We would be lost without each other.

WHITE WOMAN: And the universe has joined us together, and the universe will curse those who try to deny us, the universe will pour out her anger on those who would separate the darkness from the sun for naturalness is the order of the day. *(Takes from her pocket two onyxes. Hands one to BROTHER, puts one around his neck)* I bring you eternal darkness.

BROTHER: I bring you eternal light.

BROTHER/WHITE WOMAN:

We are one. As the morning and night are one. As life and death are one. We are one. *(They stand as they say the above.)*

WHITE WOMAN: *(Almost hysterically)* All those who move to destroy this will be damned. Shall be damned. You are warned. My focus will destroy you. *(Laughs a rasping laugh)* Now, my husband of one minute. Let us rest for a while. We need to rest. It's been a long night, hasn't it, my man.

BROTHER:	Yes. My wife of one and a half minutes. Let us rest for I gots to split and pack for the trip today. C'mon, lady, let's rest for a while.
	(BROTHER and WHITE WOMAN stretch out, she on top of him, and light fades. The SISTER is sitting on the stool. Three bags are packed. She waits. The BROTHER enters the room hurriedly. He looks somewhat tired. Disheveled. Obviously worried.)
SISTER:	Who is she? I just want to know who she is.
BROTHER:	What are you talking' 'bout?
SISTER:	*(Rises)* Who is she, mannn? Just tell me who she is? What she is? What she is that she can get you to stay out til 6 a.m. in the morning? Who is she, mannnnnn?
BROTHER:	I don't know what you're talking about.
SISTER:	I'ma talking about you mannn. I'ma talking about you leaving me here alone on our last night together. I'ma talking about you not coming to the poetry reading. I'ma talking about me anxious to get home rushing up the stairs to you. To the silence of a room, to a telephone call that told me nothing. I'ma talking about lies and more lies, I'ma talking about us, mannn. *(Moves up to his face)* Who is she, man? Is she prettier than me? Is she blacker than me? Is she taller than me? Does she make love better to you than me? I just want to know who she is.
BROTHER:	*(Coolly)* You're hysterical. Why don't you calm down? Just shut up and calm down. I told you where I was. I was taking care of some business.
SISTER:	*(Moving away with back to audience)* With whom?
BROTHER:	With someone who is organizing the trip.
SISTER:	What's her name?
BROTHER:	It's a he.
SISTER:	What's his name?
BROTHER:	What's his name? Girl, what's yo/problem? I told you

from the git go that when I'm on business, it's private. When I'm on business in the movement, it's very private. And don't be asking me. I'll tell you what I want you to know. No mo, now stop this nonsense and help me pack. I'm gon' be late for my plane.

(SISTER turns and runs over to him and hits him—the slap is loud and there is a momentary silence. Backs away.)

Don't do that again, you hear me? What you tryin' to start. You want me to beat you up so you can show everybody what a no/good/nigger I am? Is that what you want? Lookie here, baby. *(Moves to her)* Lookie here, girl, I had to leave. It was urgent business. I don't like telling you everthing cuz it could be dangerous for you and. . .

SISTER: You're lying. I know it. I feel it inside that you're lying. You got another woman. I know it. Tell me who she is, man? Is she younger than me? Is her stomach flatter than mine? *(Turning around)* What's wrong with me now? You don't like my getting big with the baby? Is that it? Why mannnnnn, why another woman, when you told me I was all that you needed. That yo/life was complete now that you had a Black woman. Were they all lies too? Just a six month year-old lie. Not even a year-old lie. Just a six/month/year-old lie. Well. That's it. I'm leaving. My bags are packed. I'm going home.

BROTHER: Just like that. *(Has moved over and poured himself a drink)* You just gonna pack up and leave. Go back to mommy and daddy so they can say/remind you every day with I told you so, I told you he was a no/good/nigger. I told you he meant you no good, him with that big Castro beard. I told you so. I told you so. And I thought you were a mature Black woman. Ready for the unknown. Ready for the fight, ready to run at the first sign of trouble. You gon' go home cuz you can't figure it all out. You don't have all the right answers.

SISTER: *(Hesitates slightly)* But this isn't the first time you've done this. This is just the first time it's been so blatant. I've gotten so many phone calls from you explaining why you couldn't come this way that I began to think you and that telephone was one. I am a Black woman, but that don't mean I should be a fool. To you being a Black woman means I should take all the crap you can think of and any extra crap just hanging loose. That ain't right, man, and you know it too.

BROTHER: Well, let's stop this now. You unpack yo/clothes. I need one of the suitcases for my trip.

SISTER: I'm going. I'm leaving you.

BROTHER: You ain't going no place.

SISTER: I'm going back to New York.

BROTHER: (Moves to suitcases and opens them, begins to throw her clothes out of cases) You ain't going nowhere now. You are officially unpacked. So jut sit down and keep quiet since you acting like such a fool. (She stands up and he pushes her back down on the stool.) Stay seated and keep quiet. I got too much on my mind to listen to this fool-ishness.

SISTER: That's the way my life is now. Scattered just like those clothes on the floor. And I'm pregnant too. What a trick bag I'm in. It's funny, you know. Don't you think it's funny, mannnn? And we ain't even legally married.

BROTHER: You sound like one of those TV/soap operas. (Sings a Hearts and Flowers song) "Tune in tomorrow and see how our dear sister turns out. When last we left her, her life was scattered out on the floor like leftover stale potato chips, pregnant, alone, unmarried, standing with her face to the sun. What more could happen to our courageous heroine? Tune in tomorrow and find out." SHEEEEET. Every time one of you bourgie bloods decide to become Black, you act like people owe you something. Well, I've been Black ALL my life. Done struggled all my life in Louisville. My mother and all her different men. All my brothers and sisters with different daddies. Girl, you don't know what hard times is all about. Just because you decided to wade into Black-ness and you found the water steaming hot from the sweat of yo/brothers and sisters, you gon' turn around and go back to N.Y.C., you bourgie/Black/bitch. Who do you think you are? Just because you're well known you think you an exception. You get what all the other Black/women of yo/time gon' git. Stand up.

(SISTER doesn't move. She's thinking quietly. He moves over and pulls her up.)

I said stand up. Who do you think you are? Just because they applaud you for some words, some poems, you say, you still gon' git what every Blk/woman's getting, you ain't no different from them at all. This is 1967. Don't you forget that. Let me help you remember who you are.

(Slaps the right side of her face)

You a Black woman bitch.

(Slaps the left side of her face)

You the same as every Black woman.

(Slaps the right side of her face)

You were born to cry in the night.

(Slaps the left side of her face)

You ain't no different from any Black woman.

(Slaps the right side of her face)

You're my mother, and my mother's mother, every Blk/man's mother I've ever seen.

(Slaps the left side of her face)

You like all Blk/women, ain't no difference.

(Then he kisses her. Long and hard)

Now. Pack my bag like I told you to. I got just a few minutes to make the plane. (SISTER picks up one bag and begins to pack the bag in silence.) Anything special you want from Mexico?

SISTER: Nothing.

BROTHER: Well, I'll choose you something nice. Hey. Maybe if Johnny and I save on some of our expenses, maybe by Friday we could send for you. How about a weekend in Mexico with yo/old/man? How would you like that?

SISTER: Yes. I'd like to be someplace with MY old man.

BROTHER: I'll see if I can work it out. Maybe with a few calls here and there, I can work it out. *(Fingers the onyx as he talks)* Yes. Maybe it can be done.

SISTER: You know, I didn't think too much about it night before last. But I had this dream. It seems that we went to the hospital together. It was time for the baby, and I had two babies, one white and one Black. I kept saying the white one wasn't mine. The hospital nurses and doctors kept smiling. No, it's yours. They said in fact we almost missed it. Thought it was the after/birth until we looked and saw this baby. It's yours. I screamed, but it's deformed. It's deformed. It's ugly. I don't want it. And their grinning faces grew bigger and bigger as they said two for one. We've got two babies for you. You can't have one without the other. That's the way it goes in this hospital. Take the two babies or none at all. I remember they were laughing as they left my room. *(Hands suitcase to the BROTHER and stands up)*

BROTHER: It's just a dream. Nothing to it. Some dreams are just weird. That's all. But sometimes, baby, you try to live too Blackly. Like giving up yo/wine and not smoking and no more pork. Girl, it don't matter what we eat as long as we do it to this man. As long as we upset his system, it don't matter what we eat.

SISTER: But we are what we eat mannnnn. And drinking is slow death. And smoking. No mo cigarettes. No mo weed for me. It's all wrong. How can we change things doing it the same way he's doing it? How can we be different being like him? Look. When some of us in New York first got our naturals people said they weren't important—that they didn't make no difference. But they have made a difference, you know. We've made people change their minds about the beauty of their hair.

BROTHER:	Aw right. I know. I know. Another time we'll argue this out. It's time for this ole dude to make it on outa here. I'll call you tonight from the hotel. Okay? And stop looking so lost. So sad. I still love you in spite of your foolishness. I forgive you. C'mon and give me a kiss.
SISTER:	*(Moves toward the BROTHER and kisses him)* Goodbye, mannnnnnnn.
BROTHER:	Maybe I'll see you on Friday night. *(Exits)*
SISTER:	*(Stands for a while and stares. Then turns around and begins to pick up her clothes. She puts them in the two bags. Then she moves/walks around the room, stopping first one place than another.)*

There must be a place for me somewhere. Let me continue walking. Ah. Here's a corner for me. *(Gets on her knees and begins to pray hesitantly)*

Oh Lord. Help me, this poor Blk/woman/sinner sitting here. Help me out of this misery. I know I have done wrong and all, but help me, dear Lord, help, yo/ poor servant here in the wilderness of California, help me. . . *(begins to laugh)* Help me to. . . *(bursts out laughing)* Girl, ain't no Lord gon' help you, at least not one that we've been taught to pray to, git off your knees. You look like some fool asking for help from one who ain't never helped Black people do anything 'cept stay on their knees. But you do need some kind of help. You made a mistake, and you don't know what to do about it. What about yo/child? What about yo/child rushing out of the darkness of yo/womb into light. You've got to give him light. Not madness. But light. What you gon' do, Black girl?

(SISTER goes over and picks up the two bags and starts out. Sits down and begins to unpack. Slowly.)

How can I go home with this big stomach? How can I? I'll forget it, that's what I'll do. I'll forget it happened and wait for him to change. He'll get over whatever she is. He'll change. He'll stop drinking. And smoking. He'll understand why a Black man must be faithful to

his woman, so she'll stop the madness of our mothers
repeating itself out loud. He just needs time. I just got
to rock myself in Blackness, insulate my soul with
righteousness and that will sustain us both. Gots to.
Yeah. *(Begins to rock back and forth)* Gots to rock myself
in Blackness. In sweet, sweet Blackness, cuz I am the
new Black woman. I will help the change to come. Just
gots to rock myself in Blackness in the knowledge of
womanly Blackness, and I shall be.

(Begins to sing a tune as she continues to rock)

> I'm a Black woman,
> gon' get Blacker than the nite become one with my
>   man.
> I'm a Black woman
> mother of the sun,
> gon' become one with my man
> and get Blacker.
> Yeah. Yeah. *(Continues to rock)*
> Gots to rock myself in Blackness
> Gots to rock myself in Blackness
> Gots to rock myself in Blackness *(Light fades to
>   Dancers)*

DANCERS: *(MALE DANCERS turn and face the audience. The two
FEMALE DANCERS, one with black mask on, the other with
white mask, sit in back—one to the right and one to the left.
MALE DANCER stands. Walks around and drinks a drink.
Turns and looks at both of them, tosses a coin to see which
one he'll visit. He walks a hip/walk to the FEMALE DANCER
wearing the black mask, holds out his hand. Kisses her and
leaves hiply. Goes to FEMALE DANCER with white mask on
and they circle each other. They're apparently equals. They
dance. He leads. Then she leads. He leads then she leads. He
leads then she leads. He finally gives up and she leads the
dance. The MALE DANCER returns to the FEMALE DANCER
with black mask and her stomach is now big, and as they
dance they can't touch till finally they're dancing without
touching each other. He returns to the FEMALE DANCER
with the white mask. He finds her stretched out lifeless on
the floor. He tries to wake her up—he drags her back and*

forth trying to wake her up. When he fails he sits and waits, and waits. She turns. She twists her body snakelike and slides up to him and curls herself round him. He is hypnotized and he begins to follow her snakelike on the floor, moving in and out finally touching. They stick out their tongues and kiss and the FEMALE DANCER with white mask becomes lifeless again. The MALE DANCER's body becomes like the sun warming her till she begins to stir again and they dance a sensuous dance. When the MALE DANCER returns to the FEMALE DANCER with the black mask on he is shaking. Chilled, tired to the bone. She greets him discordantly. Moving around dissatisfied. And he is so tired that he begins to shake. The slow movement from the feet to his shoulders and he knocks her down as he spins with each quiver of his body. He picks up his bag and moves slowly out, body twitching from the cold that he feels. The FEMALE DANCER with black mask on rolls across the floor, trying to find a comforting place. Gets on her knees and prays. First one place then another until she can clasp her hands no longer. And she laughs. Her body laughs and she becomes still. Finally she rises and straightens out her black mask. Her long dress, her natural. And she begins to march at first in a tired manner, but as she passes, she becomes upright in her Blackness and she smiles, slightly. Stage darkens.)

(There is no beginning or end.)

I'm Black When I'm Singing, I'm Blue When I Ain't

(1982)

CHARACTERS:

REENA

MAMA B

TONI (Main Female Character)

MALIKA

DOCTOR (Male)

ATTENDANT (Nurse) (Male or Female)

SAM (Mama B's Husband)

CATHOLIC MATRON (At Girl's Home)

BUSINESS MANAGER (For Mama B, Toni, and Reena) (Male)

MARY (Toni's Mother)

JOHN (Reena's Husband)

JOSEPHINE (Reena's Mother)

CHORUS/DANCERS (3 Males)

CHORUS/DANCERS (3 Females)

Place and Time:

Act I: 1980s and 1920 in Detroit, Atlanta, and New York City (NYC)

Act II: 1940s, 1960s, and present in Baltimore, Philadelphia, and NYC

ACT I

(A room—grey and white stripes—no windows. In the center of the room is a small cot; to the left is a small desk and chair. To the right is a piano. Upstage is a child's play stove with pots and pans and a play sink. Around the room there are clothes racks; on them hang dresses, hats and other costumes for actors. A woman between 40-45 years of age is stretched out on the cot. She has on a long white hospital gown with white tights. No shoes. She wears a diamond tiara, "diamond" earrings and a diamond bracelet. She is humming a tune that seems familiar. She rises. Goes to the desk

and picks up some brown paper and spreads it out on the floor, center stage. She smoothes it out. Then she squats on the paper—she is humming softly and grunting.)

REENA: *(Sings)*

> The color of death is grey and white
> The color of my life is white and grey
> They are different and yet the same
> Don't ya know—I learned all this in a cabaret

(Sings)

> The color of this room is white and grey
> The color of my mind is grey and white
> They are different and yet the same
> Don't ya know—A dog licks the hand it's gonna bite.

(Laughs/Grunts)

(She gets up from squatting and shakes herself. Then moves over to the play stove and gets a pot. Returning to the brown paper, she begins to spoon the imaginary feces into the pot. She continues to hum the aforementioned song. Then she takes it to the play stove and begins to cook. Removes the pot and goes to the cot and be-gins to eat—as she eats she glances up at the audience for the first time.) *(Extends hand)* Want Some? *(Laughs)* No, huh? It ain't too bad. It's solid you know. Don't look so shocked, we eats what we can when we can in this hellhole. *(Stands up)* But wait now. I haven't welcomed you properly my audience. My dear hard/playing/hard/paying audience. Here now. I'll straighten this part of my bed for you. *(Puts down pot)* There. It's smoothed out for you. Some of my space. Wel-come. *(Laughs and sits down)* Such as it is. *(Extends pot again)* Are you sure you don't want any? *(Laughs a gutsy laugh. Con-tinues to eat—concentrates on pot. Slowly looks up)* Don't look so disgusted. You there sitting in yo' middle-class conformity. You think I'm mad don't you. You should be grateful that I'm offering you this little shit. It's controlled shit. Institu-tionalized shit. There's so much more of it out there *(laughs)* that's running loose. And you always falling in it and always taking it too! *(She continues to eat. Looks up quickly.)* There I caught you staring again. Don't you know that's bad man-

ners? My mother always taught me the proper things to do in North Philadelphia. "Now Reena sit up straight there girl. Remember a Black girl is bad enough, but a hunch-backed-slouched-back-bad postured-back Black girl is the worst." My mother could always hit the nail right on the back. *(Laughs)*

I came from Philadelphia. Guess you've guessed that by now. I was a genius when I was a child. Do you hear? A mathematical and musical genius. Equations poured from my mouth and I square-rooted my rooms into the streets of Philadelphia. My hand took shape with music right before my eyes. I had a concert when I was four. I marched out on the concert stage, face greased, legs and arms greased, and played the old masters. This young 'un did in those old dudes. And when I finished, and when they had clapped for me and my mother, and we had bowed twenty-five times, we went home on the Broad street train together. And all she kept saying was, "I hope they didn't think you were too Black. I just hope they didn't care about that part of it." *(Laughs) (Stands)*

But momski. I had the last laugh after all. I made everybody in here, you too my dear audience, I made everybody love Black. Didn't I my little zombies. Do you remember? When I appeared on stage in all my long and thick blackness and sang:

> "I am here Black as the nite
> I am here to bring you day
> So stretch out your hand and
> I will make Blackness the way."

(Stops and turns) Ah ha—what are you looking at huh? Ah I see you looking. Yes stretch out those eyeballs saying, wait a minute, isn't that—yes that's her. They said. I mean. I heard that. . . Hee Hee Hee. You remembering me—who I am. Was. Hee, hee, hee. *(Becomes expansive)* Spirits around me. Us. Why don't you help them? They're confused by my clothes or lack of clothes. Sitting in their theater clothes. Help them. Look. They're nervous. They're thinking she was always doing so well. Why the whole country heard her first song and knew she was heading for the top. Smiling eyes and lips announced her when she walked onto a stage.

Yes. You're right. When I entered a room, music began and stopped. I walked a walk that said hunger would never populate these legs. And when the hunger came they were still eating the milk and honey of my good fortune. I ain't complaining though. But what a strange hunger those aristocrats, those well-to-do leaders of countries had. They saw me walking. Head held high. Geleed in African prints. And they convinced me that my African prints left footprints on my body. And they peeled me like a black banana, and I lay stripped, naked before the European Capitols of the world. A coat. A coat. All my songs for a coat! *(Laughs a wild laugh)* *(Moves to the cot)* *(Door opens. A CHORUS of three men enters. They have on white hospital gowns.)*

CHORUS: Our mothers die when they run naked on the land.
Ei—Ei—Ei.
We who are orphans must cry now to the world.
We have come to clean sin out of this place.
We have come to wash sin from the room.

CHORUS I: Singing your/people's praise is singing your/praise too.
But I have come to wash sin from your mouth.

CHORUS II: Are there no female heroes in the land? But I have come to beat evil from your limbs.

CHORUS III: The gates of this country are always closed to those who look like us.
Ay—ay—I have come to beat the evil out of your eyes.

CHORUS: Is the lady of the house at home? Has she forsaken us? Her children? We have come to beat the evil from the room.

CHORUS I: Move evil—from the woman's body. *(Crosses self)*

CHORUS II: Move outside all ye spirits of madness. *(Sprinkles dust)*

CHORUS III: Move away O thighs carrying death. *(Pushes against the room)*

REENA: Did you mention thighs? *(Stretches back on the cot)* Did you mention the word thighs? *(Shows stockinged thighs)* Yes. These are the thighs a woman must have to be an artist. A great artist. To earn her living as an artist. And you thought it had something to do with talent or hard work. *(Laughs)* But I wouldn't lift these thighs out of bed early in the morning though. These were evening thighs, not morning thighs. These were Parisian thighs. And Caribbean thighs. . . . *(Stops. A far away look covers her face.)*

CHORUS: *(Moves toward the cot)*

> We have come to beat out the evil from this room.
> Ay—ay—ay—Evil anywhere we find it.
> Standing straight or lying down.

(Goes to her cot and surround her—crossing themselves—moving around her bed) (She draws self up.)

REENA: You wouldn't know it when you saw it. Evil indeed! You three maniacs. You think it's so simple. You think my being here is simple. Your being here is simple? Do you know how old I am? I am 3,000 years old. I used to reside in the temples in Egypt and I wrote and sang the rites for funerals. What an honor it was to sing and write—what an honorable woman I was. What an honorable time that was. *(The door opens and the doctor and attendant enter.)*

DOCTOR: *(In white face)* Good morning Reena. How are you this morning? *(Stops. Changes. Moves back to couch)*

REENA: I'll be okay once you get these escapees from a Greek chorus out of here. Why do they always come to my room? I never invite them. Everyday they come and sprinkle me with goober dust then wait for some miracle to happen. I'm tired of them today. They make my head hurt sometimes.

DOCTOR: They're harmless Reena. They mean you no harm at all. They're really quite lovely—three lovely men for you.

REENA: Why do you say that? *(Somewhat agitated)* Why did you say three lovely men for me? Why do I need or want three? Why did you say that?

DOCTOR: Why do you think? Don't you remember our last conversation? Have you forgotten what happened?

REENA: *(Becomes agitated)* Get them out of here, do you hear? Three men indeed! Get them out of here.

ATTENDANT: *(Moves toward her with a straight jacket)* Shall I doctor?

REENA: *(Moves to confront the attendant)* Shall I what doctor? Don't you try to put that thing on me or I'll wrap it around your black ass.

ATTENDANT: Listen, I don't take no shit from . . .

DOCTOR: Leave her be. She's all right. Aren't you Reena? You're ready for your session, aren't you? *(Moves to desk and sits down)* *(REENA walks slowly to her cot. She's rather tired now and she stretches out.)*

REENA: *(Begins to sing the first song we heard at the beginning of the play)*

> The color of death is grey and white
> The color of my room is white and grey . . .

DOCTOR: Who's singing today Reena?

REENA: Yours truly Doc.

DOCTOR: Who's that Reena?

REENA: Me. Reena Malone. The one and only. There ain't another like me in the world.

DOCTOR: Yes all that's true Reena. But yesterday you introduced me to your friend. What was her name? Mama B wasn't it? *(REENA turns toward the wall. She is silent.)* Wasn't that her name? Wasn't it Mama B? Are you listening to me Reena?

REENA: Yeah. I'm listening to you Doc.

DOCTOR: Mama B was her name, wasn't it?

REENA: Maybe. But it could have been Toni too.

DOCTOR: *(Leans forward—excited)* You've never mentioned another friend. *(Writes furiously)* Why didn't you tell me this before? *(Becomes agitated)* Are you serious Reena? How do I know that you're not pulling my leg? or as you say jiving me?

REENA: *(Turns toward him)* You don't do you? That's what's so funny about all of this. You don't know for sure if I'm jiving you at all. *(Sits on edge of the cot)* Look at you. You just can't wait can you? Well you can only meet them when I want you to.

(*Stands*) They can't appear unless I will it. I'm the strongest of all of them. They just some dead ladies that didn't know how to take care of themselves. I do. I know how to protect me and my interests. Dumb bitches. Dumb black bitches. Ending up playing one nighters in one-horse towns—chitterling circuit women. I'm strictly escargots my man.

DOCTOR: Snails tonite for you Reena if you introduce me to your friend again.

REENA: (*Angrily*) I said I have two of 'em. Didn't you hear me? Which one?

DOCTOR: The one you'd like for me to meet. I'm interested in the one you'd like for me to meet now. (*Softly*) Eventually I'll meet them all.

REENA: It really doesn't matter. They're about the same. Traveling around in a car in the South. Once she even had her own railroad car. Can you imagine, traveling in those days in your own railroad car. It was painted red. A sign read Sam Reid presents: Mama B and her follies. You could see her coming as she toured the South. First class.

DOCTOR: What days are you talking about Reena?

REENA: (*Has retrieved her tiara, earrings and bracelet and has laid them out. While they talk she moves around the room and puts on a long fringe 20s type dress over the hospital gown. Should make her appear bigger. Wraps a fur piece round her neck. Places straightened wig on her head—bangs style—Plume type hat on her head.*) The good ol' days. Why them days where after a show you went to pig's feet parties. You'd walk in that door in Detroit and the funk would be flying. There it all was. Liquor. Smoke. Food. Perspiration. Fine looking Browns. Funk. And you would sit down to a steaming pot of pigs' feet, collard greens, black-eyed peas and scallions. And of course some gin. C'mon y'all, I'm ready to sing. Everybody shut up. Mama B is coming out . . .

MAMA B: My name is Mama B and I'm as brassy as can be
I say my name is Mama B and I'm as loud as I can be
C'mon over here baby and take a dip in this deep, deep
blue sea.

I was born in Chattanooga some twenty years ago
I say I was born in Chattanooga bout twenty years ago
I'm heading for NYC, don't like the South no mo'.

I got me a real pretty man who loves me down to me
toes
Say I got me a pretty man who digs me on down to my
toes
Oh how I loves that man, only the Lord hisself does
know.

I say my name is Mama B and I'm a big young brassy
one
Say my name is Mama B and I'm a big brassy one
If I ever leave my daddy baby, you can have this
Amazon.

(During this singing the DR. and ATTENDANT leave and the light-ing changes. We see REENA leaving an imaginary stage reaching for her mink and calling to her two female singers/dancers)

MAMA B: C'mon Y'all we got a recording date, Remember? Move your yellow asses. You bitches from the North think you too cute to move. C'mon today's the day we going into the recording business. Sam. Where's Sam. Can never find that man when I need him.

BUSINESS MANAGER:

(Has white side/ black side. Black side shows when speaking) I got a good deal for you Reena. You gonna record. They want you to record. Seems like Mamie done done us a favor. C'mon gal we gonna make us some money. They'll pay us $125 a side. C'mon gal. Here's a chance of a lifetime. It's big time for us.

MAMA B: *(A nervous MAMA B, young and inexperienced, enters the studio with manager.)*

"I'm fresh from the country, yuh know I'm easy to ride
Say I'm fresh from the country, yuh know I'm easy to
ride
Just climb on board me, brown skin and let me be yo
only guide

I love cornbread and milk, eat it each day I can
Say I love cornbread and milk, eat it each day I can

Promise you some of the same, if you'll be my one and only man."

Hey. Stop, y'all. I gotta spit . . . (MAMA B spits and the music stops.)

REENA: Did you see that? Did you see that loud mouth, uncouth fool? She stopped and spit in the middle of a record date. Did you see that white man's face congeal in disgust? He almost fainted. Lord Almighty. Of course, she didn't get the contract. How could she? She was too busy spitting. (Laughs)

MAMA B: (Fighting to come out) So what if I spit? I had to spit. I couldn't keep singing with all the spit in my mouth. But if those white companies didn't like me they eventually did sign me up anyway. I'm on stage now. You shut the hell up. I don't share my stage with no other blues singer when I'm on stage. That's my audience now. So you just shut your northern Philadelphia mouth up.

BUSINESS MANAGER:
(White side) It's a good deal Mama B. You'll get $3,000 a year, $150.00 a piece for the next six record dates and because we love you so much, here's a bonus of $500.00. Yes. You and Major Records are on their way. We'll do you up just fine Mama B. We even have someone to print the word colored on the record. Everybody will know who you are.

MAMA B: What you think Sam. It sound all right to you?

SAM: Best thing I've heard in a long time. We're finally on our way.

BUSINESS MANAGER:
(White side) You sign right here. On the dotted line. Just a minute. Yes? Yes sir. Right. Certainly. Right away. We don't need this line about royalties. We'll just cross it out for you. Now. Right here. Just sign on the dotted line.

MAMA B: C'mon y'all. Let's go. Sam ain't coming. And I ain't gonna sit here no longer. We'll settle up later. Atlanta here we come. Three fine looking Browns. We ready to cook. Buffet Flats here we come.

CHORUS: (Three females in men's clothes and hats)

Buffet Flats here we is
Just some quiet entertainment after all this Show Biz
So set your tables, put out your feast
We're on our way to have us some good brown meat.

CHORUS I: Time to strut Mama B. Time to stomp our feet. (*Does a dance step*)

CHORUS II: Where anything goes. Where all is discreet. (*Does a dance step*)

CHORUS III: After working six shows it's the best little retreat. (*Does a dance step*)

CHORUS: Buffet Flats, Buffet Flats here we come
Put everything you get on your serving plate
We ready to be served
And to percolate (*laughs*)

(*Music. Loud. People dancing. Couples on the bed. A low funky place. MAMA B is sitting and drinking. She's drunk by now. And loud. She gets up and tries to dance. She falls. CHORUS I falls down next to her and begins to touch MAMA B.*)

MAMA B: (*In a drunken voice*) What you want from me? Tell me what you want from me you pretty lil thing?

CHORUS I: (*Does a sensuous dance—one of rolls and turns on the floor and on her knees*)

MAMA B: (*Sings*)

Tell me, is it cuz I'm Black that you try to turn me on.
Is it cuz I'm Black that you wanna turn me on
Turn me off—yet hold me as your midnight pawn.

Tell me: Is it cuz I'm big and round that you are here
Is it cuz I'm big and round that you are here
and not there—Investigating my frontier.

Tell me: Will it matter when I'm down and out
Will it matter when I'm down and out
And not in, still I'll send me out an Injun Scout.

Tell me. Tell me. Ma Rainey was you ever this blue?
Tell me. Tell me. Mother were you ever this blue
with your gold capped teeth, did you feel this way too?

(Music fades—people leave and MAMA B is left on the floor. The CHORUS stands—dances—touches MAMA B—satisfies her.)

CHORUS I: I'm your Buffet Flats

CHROUS II: I'm your Buffet Flats

CHORUS III: I'm your Buffet Flats

CHORUS: *(Sung in counterpoint, while MAMA B sings Ma Rainey were you ever this blue)*

> We're here to serve you any ole time of day.
> Just call and we'll come and do what ever you say
> Cuz we're your Buffet Flats that walks on two cat feet
> We're you Buffet Flats that walks on two cat feet
> We're here to serve you baby any and all kind of fine
>   brown meat

MAMA B: *(Humming)* Tell me. Tell me. Ma Rainey were you ever this blue? Tell me. Tell me. Mother. Were you ever this blue. . . *(CHORUS exits.)*

REENA: You gonna be bluer than that Mama B. Here it comes. When that car hits you gonna be bluer than any midnite blue. You too drunk to feel it though. Go to sleep Big Mama. It won't hurt much longer. And you'll be safe from this country neutral with yo pain. You won't have to share any more stages. This is stage center for you. Your time is here. Put all curses aside and ride this one for free—wheeeeeee—wheeeeeee—ah—ah—ah—ah—You are dying Mama B—Ahh—I die. . . Ah, Ah—You are looking death in the face on a lonely Alabama road. Mama B. Ah Ah. I am dying. I am dying. And no one hears my death.

CHORUS: *(Males—Enter. Pick up MAMA B and carry her stretched out and they circle the stage with her)* Keloids for sale. Anyone? Keloids for sale. Anybody? Come and get your early morning keloids.

CHORUS I: Years of eating their leftovers. Finished.

CHORUS II: Nights of choking on boot-leg gin. Finished.

CHORUS III: Days of watching audiences disappear. Finished.

CHORUS: Keloids for sale. Anyone? Keloids for sale. Anybody?

Come get your early morning inheritance. . . Ladies.
(Softly) Keloids for sale. Keloids for sale—anyone?
Come get your early morning keloids. Blues/ladies.
Come get your made in America, red white and blues
keloids, ladies.

(CURTAIN)

ACT II

SCENE 1:   Present and 40s

SCENE 2:   60s and Present

SCENE I

(CURTAIN RISES)

(The cot is now center stage. All the other furniture is pulled over to the side. Small tables, chairs, piano are against the wall. Costume changes are still hanging on the wall. REENA is sitting on the cot looking at the audience. Dressed in hospital gown.)

REENA: And you thought I was mad. Didn't you? Don't you know that madness don't travel alone. It moves in crowds. And stations. Subway cars. Hotel rooms. And wayward homes for girls. Hold still. Be quiet. *(Reaching up)* I'll catch one for you. Hold still there. I'm trying to catch one for our audience sitting out there in splendid silence. They've never seen anyone catch madness in flight. *(Reaches)* There. I almost got you! *(Turns and sits down again)* And you thought I was mad. Because I was eating shit off the floor you thought that. Not me. I am who you thought I was. And if that is so, how could I be eating shit off the floor? How could I do what you thought I was not doing? Huh? There. I got you. A special kind of madness. A wayward home for girl madness. There I got you Toni and I won't let you go. You've got to tell us about those demons in penguin dress who made you cry out in the nite . . . I won't let you go . . . *(Moves around the stage. Humming the first song. Puts on a short red dress—girlish)*

CHORUS: *(Three women in long gowns) (Blue bird, blue bird thru my window. Holds REENA's hand and walks her stiffly around the room. Holds hands and won't let go.)*

TONI: Let me go. I didn't do nothing. Why I got to go to a home? He tried to do it to me. What? No. I didn't want him to. Mama. Mama. Mama. Where you at? Mama. Mama. Mama. Come get me out of this place. They gonna kill me here. Mama. Mama. Mama. Somebody speak to me. Somebody say something. I didn't do nothing. You can ask my momma. *(Blue bird—blue bird—thru my window)*

CATHOLIC MATRON:
(White face) (Walks into room) This is a good place for good girls. We don't allow evil here. The first thing we'll do is take you out of that red dress. Sinful women wear red dresses. We will purge sin out of you. You are in the Lord's house now. The Lord is thy shepherd; you shall not want here. You will be here until you're twenty-one years old. You're ten now, so you'll have a long time to get to know the almighty. Then perhaps you won't go around tempting men. *(White face)*

TONI: I wasn't tempting nobody.

CATHOLIC MATRON:
You address me as Holy Mother. Do you hear? You say yes ma'am, and no ma'am. We will cast out that pride of yours. Pride doth goeth before a fall.

TONI: Why don't you believe that I was just coming home from school and he tried to rape me? I didn't do nothing to him.

CATHOLIC MATRON:
What are you supposed to say? I won't say it again. You respect the authority here or else. Now once more. You address me as Holy Mother. I am your link with God while you live here.

TONI: But I didn't do nothing. Where's my mama. She don't mean to leave me here.

CATHOLIC MATRON:
Your mother is good. She agrees with us. She knows that you need to be raised in a Godly way. Your wildness is painful to her.

TONI: You lie. Mama she love me. I don't be lying to her. I went wild. I just like to listen to them records in the houses I clean. It's pretty music.

Sin. Thy name is sin girl. We will wash sin from your eyes. Your ears. Your mouth. No songs shall move your lips other than the songs of God. Come and get her. Take her away until she apologizes for her sullenness. *(TONI runs toward the matron and spits in her face. CHORUS grabs her)*

CHORUS: *(Three women in Catholic garb) (Blue bird—blue bird—toss her back and forth.)* Here she is children. Another player. But this is a bad one.

CHORUS I: You mustn't talk to her, till she apologizes.

CHORUS II: You mustn't talk to her, till she apologizes.

CHORUS III: You mustn't talk to her, till she apologizes.

CHORUS I: Maybe she'll do like the other one.

CHORUS II: Push herself higher and higher in the swing.

CHORUS III: Until it breaks and she flies screaming to her death.

(They push TONI out of the circle—they run laughing from the room like Black vultures.) (The scene goes dark. TONI moves forward on the stage and sits.)

TONI: Ain't never liked the dark. Always feels like its choking me. Always feels like my grandmother's arms that nite I woke up. Her dead and all. Her arm strangling me. And it dark and all. So what if they don't talk to me. So what if they leave me in red cuz I'm a sinner. I'm gonna sit right here and not move. I'm gonna sit right here and wait for momma. She always remembers me at some point. And we'll go far away from these old biddies and have a nice place to live. And we'll have plenty to eat. And she'll rock me like she useta when I was little and afraid of the dark. I'm 10-years-old and I ain't afraid of no dark. *(Begins to sing a children's song)*

> Ain't no boogieman a—t—all
> Ain't no kinda spooks or haints
> Ain't nothing but the nite
> Searching for his blessed saints.
> Ain't no owls hooting at me
> Ain't no roots at my door.
> Ain't nothing but the night
> Trying to touch me on this floor.

(She becomes bolder. Sits on knees. Puts hands on hips and sings tauntingly.)

> Ain't no boogieman a—t—all
> Ain't no kinda spooks or haints
> Ain't nothing but the night
> Searching for his blessed saints

(Laughs out loud)

CHORUS: *(3 nun/like/women)*

> We've had mercy on you my child
> We've brought you a playmate
> Hold out you hands and greet her
> We have come to consecrate.

CHORUS I: In the beginning there was the word.

CHORUS II: And it sounded like a mockingbird

CHORUS III: In the beginning there was no word.

CHORUS I: And it looked like a little blackbird.

CHORUS:

> One, two, three, she sees you
> Four, five, six, what will you do?
> Seven, eight, nine and ten
> By the way, her name is Gwen

CHORUS I: Gwen this is Toni

CHORUS II: Toni this is Gwen.

CHORUS III: Gwen Toni's ten

CHORUS I: Toni, Gwen's a big fat hen.

(They exit laughing. They leave a body wrapped in a blanket.)

TONI: It is getting cold. Do you mind if I use part of your blanket Gwen? It's okay. They're gone. We can talk now. We can beat these old biddies at their own game. My momma always say when a woman that mean it means she needs a man. Hey Gwen. You awake? Could I have some more of your covers? Why don't you talk girl. It's okay. Don't nobody come back this way this time of nite. Gwen. *(TONI shakes her and Gwen rolls over dead. TONI stands up and screams. Bangs on the door.)*

Somebody help me. Somebody come and help me. She dead. You hear me? She dead. Help. I promise to be good. Ma'am. I promise to be good. You hear me ma'am. She dead. Mamma. Mamma. Mamma. Help. Help me Mamma. They got me locked up in this room with a dead girl. I can't get out Mamma. I won't be bad no mo! I won't sass you none. I'll give you all the money I make washing those steps. Just please c'mon and help me tonite. *(Continues to bang on door. Bangs the entire nite.)* *(Stage lightens. Bangs on door. TONI is sucking her hands. Licking the blood away but by the time she gets up, she's a young lady. No longer a child. Begins to change the room. Pulls chairs and tables out to make a small nite club.)*

CHORUS: *(Three men carry three signs. They carry and read their signs.)*

CHORUS I: "A nice colored woman who can cook and typewrite for $35.00 a month."

CHORUS II: "A Nice light—skinned woman for domestic work. Under Thirty-five-years old. $30.00 a month, room and board."

CHORUS III: "Only pretty, light-skinned girls need apply. Chorus girls. Salary depends on experience. Any experience."

TONI: Please give me a chance mister. I just walked from 145th Street to 133rd Street. Just give me a chance. If it don't work then I'll walk on out the do'. *(Walks over to the piano player)* You know this one? *(Sings)*

> "I'm tired of being up on a shelf
> tired of walking all by myself
> Got nobody for my lonesome self.
> Where is he who'll come my way
> Hold my hand til the break of day
> Got nobody going my way.
> I say I'm tired of being up on a shelf
> Tired of walking all by myself
> Got nobody for my lonesome self. *(Repeat)*

MANAGER: *(Black face)* You got a job. $18.00 a week. Plus tips. You got quite a voice there. Think we'll go far together. What's your number for my records?

CHORUS: *(In showgirl costumes)* At the Harlem club we do our stuff. Just walking around and strutting our stuff. The manager says when they hand out tips we got to pick it up with our bottom lip. *(Shakes the bottom of body)*

CHORUS I: Here's a nice colored girl with great big lips.

CHORUS II: Here's a fine brown skin, with no fingertips.

CHORUS III: C'mon Toni, go on and do your dips.

CHORUS:
> We make more money this way
> Moving our bottoms each and everyday
> C'mon Toni give it a kick
> It ain't like turning a trick

TONI: That's not part of my job. I sing here. And nothing else. All the extra crap is for the birds. Hey. You don't have to do that you know. You get paid to dance and sing. We ain't gotta do that.

CHORUS: *(Dresses TONI as they sing)*

> Sez who? Who you a countess or something
> May be a famous lady
> Who you a duchess or something
> Maybe a well/known/lady.

CHORUS I: Sez who? I need the job so I'll do what they say.

CHORUS II: Sez who? I need the job so I'll follow and play.

CHORUS III: Sez who? I need the job so I'll oil my lips each day.

CHORUS:
> Cuz we ain't no countess like you
> We ain't no duchess lady like you
> We're just some poor brown skins
> Tryin to make it thru.

CHORUS I: All right your highness here's your crown.

CHORUS II: Your highness, your highness. Your white gown.

CHORUS III: You already own all of uptown.

CHORUS I: Let's try that society way downtown.

BUSINESS MANAGER:
(White side) Got you a contract down here. You won't have to worry about segregated rooms. This is my downtown. Got you $72.00 a week for 2 years—7 nites a week. You're big now

Countess—your Highness the world awaits you. You're on top of the world.

TONI: (*Sings*)

My name is Antoinette
I'm as fine as mellow wine
I pay my rent and walk my dog
Own everything that's mine.
I'm a good hearted woman
Say I'm good right down to the bone
Go home each nite at midnite
I'm never out on loan.
Yes my name is Antoinette
And my head is screwed on tight
I don't eat cake, I just eat bread
Don't have a great big appetite.
I'm a good hearted woman
Say my prayers each and every nite
I get right down on my knees
And thank the lord for you each nite

MARY: (*Walks on stage. A small woman. Still very beautiful*) You should wait Toni. Learn more about that man. He's too pretty. A pretty man only bring you pain. I know. I've had plenty a pretty men and what did it get me. Always walking down streets, looking in bars for them. Get someone respectable. A business man, a lawyer or plumber. No musician baby. No pretty musician baby. They hard luck for womens. They have all kinds of bad habits baby. I want the best for you baby.

TONI: Momski. He love me like I love him. I've only loved two people in my life, you and Bill. Don't ask me to stop loving him. I want to love both of you equally. Give me a chance. Give us a chance.

MARY: Play it by ear baby. Listen for the discordant notes too. You don't have to read notes to know if the music is sweet or not. Listen. Your ear is trained; now train your eyes girl. I want you to be happy. You're making $1,000 on 52nd Street. Don't throw it away. Don't throw your peace away for some romantic dream. (*During this talk TONI has moved backstage and gotten her diamond tiara. Puts on her diamonds and leans against the piano—now almost center stage too.)*

TONI: *(Sings)*

> Why do they put our mommas always in the kitchens?
> Why do they hang our daddies from the highest tree?
> Why do they tell us all to wait for the judgment day?
> Why are we waiting, waiting to be free?
> If you wanna be free, you gotta take your freedom
> If you gonna be free, you'll have to take it
> So walk right up to Uncle Sam and say
> I'm here to take my freedom today.
> Why do they put our mommas always in the kitchens?
> Why do they hang our daddies from the highest tree?
> Why do they tell us all to wait for the judgment day?
> Why are we waiting, waiting to be free?
> *(Softly)*
> Why are we waiting to be free?
> Why are we waiting to be free?

(TONI turns and goes to the hangers. She pulls off dress and puts on hospital gown. Straps her diamonds, money to her legs. Goes over to the child's stove and heats pan. Brings it over to the bed and begins to shoot up. Stretches out and falls back.)

CHORUS: *(3 males in hospital gowns)*

> It's so sweet when it hits you
> It feels like morning dew
> It's so goooodd when it warms you
> It thrills you through and through

CHORUS I: Look at the Countess. She's given up her throne.

CHORUS II: Look at her highness. She's white at the bone.

CHORUS III: Look at the duchess, no place to call her own.

CHORUS I:
> Who will succeed her?
> Who will take her place?
> We need another one like Mama B
> or Toni. Who'll inherit her space?

(They circle her and take her diamonds—exit.)

REENA: *(Leans up. Smiles)* She was short termed. You dudes knew that. Dead. So early. So young. But so stupid. She didn't know how to hold herself. You've got to support yourself against the silences of the world. That's how my momma paid me back when I did something wrong. Silence. Long cold blue silences. I can hear them now. That's how my husband paid me back. Long red silences. He'd shoot them cross our rooms until I burned. John and Josephine what a team.

(JOHN and JOSEPHINE enter holding hands. REENA freezes.)

JOSEPHINE: You're not going to wear your hair like that. Nappy? No comb in it. Girl what are you doing to yourself?

JOHN: That's a stupid dress you're wearing today Reena. Take it off. Put on the black one. You're too black to wear white well.

JOSEPHINE: When are you going to play the classics again? You were trained for the classics, not all this black stuff.

JOHN: You're drinking too much Reena. And I'm taking the pills from you too. You look terrible. Why don't you rest awhile? One more word out of you and I'll kick your ass. You're Queen of nothing in this house. You better stop those airs you put on with those adoring fans. I'm your ole man and I have no problem with kicking your black ass if you keep messing with me.

JOSEPHINE: Where is the child? What kind of mother are you anyway? How can you take care of her properly if you're always on the road? *(Walks over to REENA)* And you have such pretty hands. A concert pianist hands, not this junk you're playing. You are an artist. *(Looks at REENA)* Why don't you put some powder on? Some white powder. It makes you look so Black with nothing on your face.

REENA: *(Rises from the cot. Begins to scream)* Ai—Ai—Ai—Momma. Momma. Momma. Why didn't you ever love your tall black daughter? And you. My teacher. Lover. Wasn't I beautiful enough for you? You two deserve each other. Go on walk on out of here. Holding hands like lovers. Conspirators against me. Get out of my life both of you. I don't need none of you. Cuz I'm Reena the Long Black Lady of Soul. *(Begins to sing)*

They'll try to kill us all
We must take a stand
They'll try to color us dead
We must have a master plan
Raise up the children. Do you hear?
To walk a righteous walk
Tell them they're Black and Beautiful
And listen to them talk
Cuz: We are Black
Blacker than the nite
Blacker than the History we've tried to forget
Cuz: We are Black
And we will show the world
Black is the beginning of everything.
I said—Did you hear me?
Black is the beginning of everything . . . *(Repeat)*

Thank you Cheri. I'm gonna leave this country. Leave America. It'll kill us all. I'm going to Africa First. Then Europe. Then the Caribbean. There are people there who love me, who'll take care of me, who tell me I have the most beautiful body on this earth. What do you think? It is beautiful isn't it? Trinidad. I love Trinidad at carnival time. Hey it's carnival time. *(Opens up hospital gown—she has on a bikini.)* Hey it's carnival time. Trinidad

CHORUS: *(Three men in costumes of grey and white)*

Carnival time. Time to relax. And Be.
Let your hair down. Have some fun. And Be.
Carnival time in Trinidad. Come on. And Be.

CHORUS I: Hey there. Yankee gal. Where's your costume? *(Laughs)*

CHORUS II: Hey there. Is your costume your perfume? *(Laughs)*

CHORUS III: Hey child. Who you be dressing for? For whom? *(Laughs)*

CHORUS: Carnival. It's carnival time. Do you want to?
We won't stop you. Ain't nothing here taboo.
Take off your clothes. And be our beautiful Zulu.

(The dance. REENA dances an African dance and the men dance around her with her, until they all fall out in the streets of Trinidad. They stir and pick her up and spread her legs and bring her

back to her cot. They pull her every which way like scavengers then drop her on the bed. And exit.)

SCENE II

(REENA is sitting at the piano. The DOCTOR is sitting at the desk. The ATTENDANT is leaning against the wall.)

DOCTOR: What do you mean you're having difficulty playing, Reena? The piano is tuned.

REENA: It's not that. I just can't control what music comes out of my fingers.

DOCTOR: I don't understand what you mean.

REENA: Listen Doc. *(She begins to play a soft, sentimental ballad. Then a violent piece. A progressive classical piece comes out like Cecil Taylor. She pulls her hands away quickly.)*

DOCTOR: What wrong with that music Reena? It sounds beautiful— aggressive but beautiful.

REENA: It's not my music. It's hers.

DOCTOR: Who is that? Mama B? Toni?

REENA: No, her. The one who calls herself Malika.

DOCTOR: Why does she play like that Reena?

REENA: She's just trying to annoy me—that's all. I've told her if she continues to do this that I will send her back. I told her to be cool.

DOCTOR: Suppose she doesn't intend to stop. Suppose she doesn't intend to go back. What then?

REENA: *(Stands)* I'm in control here, Doc. Don't you or that sloppy attendant forget that? I know what I'm doing. I've always kept them under control haven't I?

DOCTOR: Yes you have. But suppose this one is smarter? What then? Suppose she's not from the past. What kind of name is that anyway?

REENA: That's not possible . . . I . . . I . . . *(Grabs her throat as if she's choking)* No . . . No . . . I . . . don't . . . want . . . to . . . hear . . . you.

MALIKA: Reena. I want to come out. You can't stop me.

REENA: No, I'm the main one here. I'm stronger than all of you together.

MALIKA: I've talked to the others. And they agree with me. They've decided to rest now, Reena. They know it's time to rest and that it's me, Reena. Your time has come and gone. Let me out peacefully, Reena.

REENA: No. I'm here to stay. You can't control me. I am here to stay. *(Begins to parade around the room)* Look. I come from a History of strong women. What/who are you? You some weak, light/skinned bitch trying to take over? You probably can't even sing. Now can ya?

MALIKA: Reena. Listen, my sister. I'm not trying to replace you. I just want to continue you in a newer form. It's time for you to sit down and rest. Your songs have run out.

REENA: I won't. I can't. They still love me in the world. In Europe. I'm going to Paris next week. I'm due in Senegal in two weeks. Who can sing a song like me? Who else can tell you about love and loneliness? Mississippi and Alabama? How dare you think about forgetting me? Pushing me out of the limelight. *(Moves front stage.)* All you niggers are just alike. Always trying to wipe someone out.

MALIKA: I'm coming out Reena. Move over.

          (A battle ensues—one where REENA and MALIKA fight standing up.)

REENA: *(Doubles over in pain then gets control again)* Got you that time Bitch. *(Walks queenly like)* I'm traveling to Paris next week.

          (Doubles over in pain)

MALIKA: I will rework this arm, this leg so no more needles riddle them.

REENA: *(Gains control again)* You didn't know I was that strong did you? I'm traveling to Switzerland tomorrow. *(Doubles over in pain)*

MALIKA: I will restring these eyes so beauty falls from them like diamonds.

REENA:	I got you pinned now. I got you now. *(Moving around back to the bed. Fall on the bed.)*
MALIKA:	I will rethread your tongue with silken words.
REENA:	*(Bouncing back and forth on bed)* I'll hit you in the stomach/ mouth anywhere bitch.
MALIKA:	*(Rocking in Blackness in the bed)* I will rock you in Blackness so you will grow to love yourself. *(Begins choking self)*
REENA:	*(Stands up on bed)* I won. Look Doc. I won. She don't know where I come from. I come from death that sparkles with her innuendos. I come from men who cry in the nite. I come from midnite streets in Philadelphia. *(Laughs)* It's carnival time! C'mon y'all. It's carnival time.
CHORUS:	*(Men) (Comes out calling)* Carnival man. It's carnival time.
CHORUS I:	Where our Yankee girl?
CHORUS II:	Where our carnival girl?
CHORUS III:	Where our hiding Yankee girl?
REENA:	*(Bows down in pain. CHORUS leaves—scared)*
	Ay—Ay—Ay—Ay—Momma. They trying to destroy me. My own people are trying to kill me. Momma. Momma.
CHORUS I:	*(Women) (Walking 'cross stage) (Walking together)* I am yo' Momma Reena. And your sister and yo' Momma.
REENA:	They trying to kill me Momma. Help.
CHORUS II:	You can never die Reena. You will live forever in me.
REENA:	But never to sing again. Never to hear applause again.
CHORUS III:	*(Backs REENA up)* My applause will be yo' applause. They will be clapping for you and me. When I hear it, I'll say Reena. Listen. They are applauding us.
REENA:	*(Laughs. Moves to center of stage)* You'll see. It don't mean nothing just to say you Black. If you don't have nothing to back it up.
CHORUS I:	It'll mean something to say you're Black when you teach Black people to back it up.

REENA: *(Picks up scarf)* It don't mean nothing to wear your Black, if you have no place to change when you need to.

CHORUS II: It'll mean something to wear your Black when every Seam is in place for you and me. *(Exits)*

REENA: *(Center stage. Challenging to audience—she talks like a poem.)*

> I came to you—long and Black
> Knew this face was ugly and sad
> I came to you when the rhetoric of the time
> Pushed me to say Blackness was bad, bad, bad!
> I came to you saying look at me, look at me
> Set me free from years of hating my face
> From the pain of years of hating myself
> And my words got stuck in the sounds of your embrace.
> *(To be sung)*
> You said you loved me, but you didn't
> You just loved my words and not really me
> You said you loved my Blackness but you didn't
> And I got lost inside myself just trying to be.
> What I could never be
> What you never thought could be me
> What we both knew wasn't me
> And I got lost inside myself just trying to be
> What I could never be
> What you never thought could be me
> What we both knew wasn't me. . .

REENA: *(Turns to audience)* I just wanted you to know my pain. I just wanted you to hear my pain. Malika—where are you girl? You've been here all along. C'mon out girl. I want to know something. Can you sing bitch? Can you sing like we all used to sing, bitch? Cuz then you won't really ever be Blue when you singing to them and they reach out to you and the words come and all is fine—fine as mellow wine. . . .

MALIKA: I'm here Reena. Waiting.

REENA: See ya later alligator.

MALIKA: After awhile crocodile.

REENA: Eat your supper.

MALIKA: Motha fucka

REENA: Tough titty

MALIKA: You old Black/Kitty

REENA: Who you calling old Bitch? *(Laughs)* Slap me five.

MALIKA: Don't take no jive

REENA: See you later alligator

MALIKA: After awhile crocodile. *(Folds scarf—dances. Puts REENA away—under piano and dances back—turns.)* **See you later alligator. After awhile crocodile.**

MALIKA: *(á la Abbey Lincoln)*
          (Talks—drums are low here)

          The earth turns old and sits staring at us
          Wondering what next we'll say and do
          We sit waiting for someone to speak
          Our minds are on a midnite curfew
          We fear talking out loud to each other
          We're afraid to admit that the time has come
          We see what things are like today and know that this
          Silence has made us dumb
          (Sings—chants)
          Aren't you tired of the tears?
          Black people/aren't you tired of the fears
          Black people/you know the days are long
          Nites longer/when you continue to hold your tongue
          I heard him crying in the nite, didn't ya?
          Momma, momma, they got me momma, they got me
          I heard her coughing blood in the nite
          Ay—ay—ay—I'm cold Momma
          I'm dying Daddy. Didn't ya?
          And Mama B sweating her Black heard her
          And Toni pulling her skin heard him
          And Reena shouting obscenities at the world heard her
          Didn't ya?
          We've got to change the sound of our kin
          From Fear, Silence, Screams in the nite to
          Oooh—oooh—ay—ay—yee—ya—ya

Oooh—ay—ay—ya—ya
Oooh—oooh—oooh—oooh—Ho

(She does a warrior dance. Employing arms and legs—she kicks to the left and three men—CHORUS—bop across the stage. She kicks to the right—chanting. They stop. Come to her and pick up and dance to chant with her—warrior style. Two women—CHORUS—come twittering across the stage. The group kicks to the left and then to the right. They stop and come and join and dance together. The other members of the cast come from behind the curtains and dance steps—and do African screams. After the cast comes on, they dance one more sequence and freeze with their hands in fists.)

(LIGHTS OUT)

2 X 2

(2009)

CHARACTERS:

BEVERLY SMITH: Mother and Grandmother
RAMONA SMITH: Daughter and Mother
JAMAL (17 year old)
NIA (14 year old)
SHAQUILLE (6 year old)

We see them only through their voices and quick movements on the stairs.

PLACE: *The living room of Beverly Smith/with stairs*
           The living room of Ramona Smith/with stairs
           A screen hangs at the back of the stage.

CURTAIN RISES:

Two people are sitting on stage—Beverly and Ramona Smith. They are sitting apart from each other in separate chairs. Beverly Smith faces the audience. Ramona sits with her back to the audience. There is a large screen at the back of the stage. A coat rack stands between them with 3 hats: a graduation hat, and two wool hats.

BEVERLY: The morning opened with such grace today. As i swept the porch this morning, i was filled with a sense of well-being. There was a song, i think, rising from the streets. The sounds coming from the street rhymed like poetry. *(Begins to hum)*

(JAMAL moves up the stairs.)

BEVERLY: Jamal, you up already, huh? You came in very late last night— you can't keep hanging out with your "posse" and keep up with your college prep classes at Temple.

JAMAL: *(Moving up the stairs)* Mama, would you wake me up in one hour? i'll be on time, i promise. i won't miss your precious Temple University classes. Just had some important business to take care of last night.

BEVERLY: i was watching that young woman out there again today. She was cleaning off the new mural again. She'll never finish it if it keeps getting marked up at night. Can't figure it out. Why it's happening—didn't the neighborhood ask for a mural, Jamal?

JAMAL: (*Goes up—stands at the top of the stairs*) People got to learn what belongs to them and what don't. (*Laughs*).

BEVERLY: Well, you can't keep going out every night. You still in school at Temple, and you still working at SuperFoods. You'll never get enough sleep.

JAMAL: (*Silent*)

BEVERLY: Well i'm gonna go over to your mama's house today. Gonna bring Nia and Shaquille back here this evening. i spoke to your mama. She don't sound so good. She sounds like she's in trouble again. She. . .

JAMAL: (*Still at top of the stairs*) i don't want to hear anything about her, you hear? i haven't seen her—spoken to her in over a year. Don't want to hear nothing she has to say. . . (*mumbles*). Dumb bitch.

BEVERLY: i won't let you disrespect your blood, boy. Your mama wasn't always the way she is today.

JAMAL: (*Turns on the stairs toward BEVERLY*) Mama, i don't want to hear about who she was and what she was like. What i know about her is that she left me on too many streets at night. i was cold, hungry too many days. What i know about her is that she loves only one thing. Not you. Not me. Not Shaquille. Not Nia. She loves crack. Crack. You hear me. i'm just surprised that she's got those kids back from their daddy.

BEVERLY: Jamal. Baby. When you're older you will understand how life just turns us around sometimes, away from. . . away from those who love us. Away. . . even from loving yourself.

JAMAL: Don't wanta talk about her, Mama. Got to get upstairs—before my classes.

BEVERLY: How are your classes, Jamal? Are they helping you get ready for college?

JAMAL: They a snap, Mama. Glad you made me go though. Glad you came and got me years ago. You saved my life. Yeah, Mama. Get those kids outa there. Bring 'em on over here. We'll take care of them. She'll let them see things their eyes ain't got no business seeing. Go get 'em, Mama.

BEVERLY: *(Watches him disappear up the stairs. She stands and turns the chair sideways. She's on a bus, looking out the window as it moves through downtown Philadelphia—as the bus passes City Hall, she closes her eyes. There are pictures on the screen of young high school students marching downtown—with signs. They all have big naturals. They are surrounding City Hall. They chant: we demand it—Black Studies, Black History, Black Literature, Black books. More Black teachers. The police come rushing toward them with billy clubs—she sees RAMONA holding her sign. She's pushed down— pushed toward the van. The students are still chanting; many are running. They're caught—herded like cattle. A picture of Rizzo, the police commissioner, smiling. And today, yesterday becomes blurred as BEVERLY exits the bus. Turns chair towards RAMONA.)*

RAMONA: *(Turns her chair to face the audience—she's a young RAMONA. She stands up.)* Mama Mama Mama. We did it. C'mon Tyrone, hurry up; you're so slow. Mama, we did it. We shut down City Hall. We chanted/ told them what we wanted. Oh Mama. A river—a river of girls and boys running on Broad Street. There was no sun out—we didn't need it. We were shining on Broad Street. Oh Mama, i felt beautiful. Felt like i had drunk holy water *(laughs)* or something. We took on this big city called Philadelphia. We said: listen to us, your children. We were so happy. Give us Black Studies. Give us something about our history in these schools. . . .Oh we were shining saints. Anointed. . . .And then we saw your face. You looked at us with such fear. Your eyes went back in your head. Your mouth stopped talking. You lost your breath. You sat still. Didn't say a word. And it was, i think, the fear in your eyes that made us stop our celebration. Then we got excited again, continued to explain our minds, our victory. And you just sat down on the couch. All the time not saying a word—just staring at us like we were strangers. Aliens. And the fear oozed out of your pores, and we smelled it. And we finally sat down too and met your fear face to face. . . . *(Turns chair away from the audience)*

BEVERLY: *(Turns her back to the audience)* Nia. Are you there? Shaquille are you upstairs? it's Mama. i need for you two to go get cleaned up. i'm taking you back to my house. is your mother upstairs?

NIA: *(With SHAQUILLE on the stairs at RAMONA's house)* She ain't here. You know she ain't here, Mama. She ain't been here for 3 days.

BEVERLY: Well i'm going to start putting up things and washing these dishes in the kitchen. i'll make you some breakfast if i can find anything to cook down here.

SHAQUILLE: Mama, how about some grits? Make us some eggs and grits.

NIA: There ain't no eggs, stupid. We ate the last eggs up two days ago. You so stupid, Shaquille. Don't you remember anything? We got some cereal, Mama. That's about all. Just some damn cereal, no milk—maybe some powdered milk that tastes like snot.

BEVERLY: Nia, stop your cussing. Stop calling your brother stupid, too. You weren't raised to do any cussing.

NIA: Raised? You mean when we were with you? We aren't raised here, Mama. Who's raising us. My mother? Your daughter? i'm raising Shaquille here in this house. i wash his clothes. Cook his food. Help him do his homework. i fix his breakfast, lunch and dinner if there's any food. i open the door when she bangs on it late at night cuz she's left her keys some place. i fight off her boyfriends' hands trying to touch me. i ain't little no mo, Mama. *(Moves to the top of the stairs)* i'm 14 years old, and i take care of everything in this god damn beat up house—that has no heat. No food. No love. No nothing in it. Just shadows.

BEVERLY: Just go get dressed, Nia. We'll talk when you get downstairs. Help your brother to get dressed, OK? And pack whatever you can. Even the dirty clothes. i'm taking you home with me today.

NIA: She'll just come and get us. Swear she's straight. Swear she's clean again. And you'll let her take us cuz she'll cry and hug you, Mama, like before. i'm not going unless it's forever. You hear me? Tired of going back and forth like some ping pong ball. i want some peace, Mama. i wanna be normal like other girls. Laugh sometimes just to laugh. i need some peace.

BEVERLY: Just get your things together now. i promise you it'll finally be all right. We gonna manage all of this—you'll have some peace. *(Turns chair toward RAMONA)* i didn't know.

RAMONA: i told you.

BEVERLY: i mean i didn't know.

RAMONA: Yes, you did, Mama. i told you.

BEVERLY: i mean i didn't hear you. i didn't understand what you were saying.

RAMONA: Yes, you did, Mama. You said, finally, sit down. Sit still. You said, don't move, girl. Boy. Sit still, you said.

BEVERLY: i didn't know what you came home from that day.

RAMONA: Yes, you did, Mama. We brought light and noise—it blinded you and scared you. All you wanted was peace.

BEVERLY: i didn't like the hair—so big and nappy. i didn't like the Blackness—so bold. i kept saying we are Negroes, not Black. Negroes. if you keep this up, i'm gonna put you out of this house.

RAMONA: And i sat still and the dust of North Philadelphia began to choke me and i coughed and coughed and coughed until your rhythm surrounded me and i made it my rhythm.

BEVERLY: Later on—you seemed happy, though too quiet. You seemed ready to paint a canvas—a joy in our living room. i remember you came home one day from school and your eyes were shaking light again. i thought you were happy.

RAMONA: i found the secret of life. *(Laughs)*

BEVERLY: i'm remembering your face that day. i could hear Jesus in your and Tyrone's voices. it scared me, baby. Jesus didn't belong in no demonstration—in all of that noise you brought into the house.

RAMONA: It scared me too, but it held back the death in North Philadelphia.

BEVERLY: *(The front door opens—hears her daughter's voice.)* Ramona, i'm in the kitchen, washing the dishes, cleaning the kitchen. Can i speak with you a minute?

RAMONA: *(Enters kitchen. She once was a striking, beautiful woman; now her eyes are dull. Face swarthy and muddy. She is too thin. RAMONA and BEVERLY turn their chairs toward each other.)* How long have you been here, Mama?

BEVERLY: Long enough to know it's time to take these children outa here. Get rid of your friends. We need to talk.

RAMONA: Oh, i see. *(Laughs)* The good mother has come. The grandmother arrives to rescue the children from their terrible mother.

RAMONA: *(Calls out to the people in the living room, says she'll see them later)* So what's the deal, mama? You gon just walk in here and take them on over to West Philadelphia? The way you did Jamal— huh? From one ghetto to another—huh? *(Laughs)*

BEVERLY: i know i ain't got much, Ramona. But they'll have the right environment, the right food. And above all a little peace. Children need a little peace from all the wars around them.

RAMONA: You know where i was today, Mama? Remember Tyrone, my friend? Remember Tyrone, who was a part of our demonstration that day, remember? He was short, stubby, and funny. Always laughing, cracking us up with some joke. But he was so brave. He stood in front of me so i didn't get hurt real bad. So brave. So funny. Well, Mama. Tyrone stopped laughing today. He just decided to parachute himself in front of a train. Just stood there, someone said, waited for the train to come into the station, and he jumped. No words. No sounds. No note. No goodbyes. Guess he couldn't take this running on those lost legs no more. He just met death on a North Philadelphia Station. *(Laughs)* Maybe that's what i should do, Mama—just jump. Put you and the children out of your misery. if i jump, if i parachute myself outa here, do you think i'll meet my young self again? *(Laughs)*

BEVERLY: i know all of this ain't your fault, girl. i know it's been hard for you at times. Maybe if i take some of the pressure offa you, you can get yourself together. Get into another program to help you get your priorities straight. You still young you know. You still got time.

RAMONA: Time. Time? *(Laughs)* What kinda time i got Mama? Time's passed me by. There was a time though that i was on time. i rode time like it was my lover. Mama. There was music in my eyes Mama. You didn't see it though. There was a dance poem in me and my friends as we raised our voices against this oppression and some people listened. And yes. . . some of us were arrested and those cops felt our young girl flesh. But you Mama. When i walked in this same door triumphant with Tyrone, proud laughter spilling out the corners of my mouth. You stopped it. You made me feel that all that we were doing was wrong. Mama. You took away my pride, my pulse. My safe sound that i had found amid all of this decay in North Philadelphia. You made me feel like nothing. All you could say wuz that education was the key. Education was the key. We had to stop this demonstrating for this Black stuff. Education would free us. Free me? Whose education?

BEVERLY: *(Moving chair closer)* i didn't understand what y'all were trying to do. i have been raised to be quiet you know. Make no noise at all about anything. To respect the law. And your father had died the year before. . . but you right. i should have listened to my child. My one and only child—so caught up in everything Black. . . .But i think i now understand some of what i didn't understand with you. Jamal is doing something in the neighborhood—He's challenging one of the smartest. Each day she paints that mural and each night he desecrates it paints graffiti all over it. i'm not stopping him you know. i mean i'm letting him do what he thinks is right. Not what i think. Yesterday on his way to school he said—they can't mess with our memorials Mama. They part of our struggle out here to live. Sacred spaces. i know i should have done the same thing with you girl. And i can say i'm sorry to your face now. i'm sorry that i was so full of fear. That i let it keep you from listening to your own music.

RAMONA: Mama. Thank you. That's the first time you said you're sorry. i'm sorry too Mama.

BEVERLY: i'm sorry i made you sit still.

RAMONA: i'm sorry for hating you and myself all these years.

BEVERLY: i'm sorry i made you fearful.

RAMONA: i'm sorry i aged you so Mama.

BEVERLY: i'm sorry i didn't let you dream.

RAMONA: i'm sorry that i gave up on myself and didn't have your strength.

BEVERLY: i'm sorry i didn't let myself dream.

RAMONA: i'm sorry i have forgotten my name. Your name. Their names. Take them outta here Mama. Take them outta here—away from their mother whose anger will break them in two. Take them outta here Mama until i can remember us again. Keep them outta here.

BEVERLY: You don't remember when your father and i broke up—probably not. You were six years old and he began a relationship with one of his coworkers in the post office. i usta follow him around—spy on them. Caught them in a hotel room together. i went after him and he just held me back—pinned me down— all the time laughing at me. i can still hear his laughter. And i sat in that hotel room after they both left and cried. i must have fallen asleep because when i awoke it was after midnight—i had left you with Mrs. Jones down the corner from us—when i showed up you were asleep and i carried you home—and i sat up all nite planning how i would get revenge. i put him out the house. Called him every name i could think of. And he left, moved in with her. They lived in West Philadelphia. When summer came i took you to Aunt Beatrice's place in Maryland. i just deposited you and left you there. i never looked back but i heard you calling my name: Mommie. Where you going? Mommie. Don't leave me. Mommie. And i kept walking. Caught the train back to Philadelphia. i worked at the hospital and partied every night. i caressed more bar stools than i want to remember. i got pregnant—went to a friend's house. Had an abortion. Not a good doctor. Developed a bad infection. When George and i reconciled two years later, we tried to have another child. i never told him the reason why we couldn't have any more children. So don't think i'm so strong. i'm just older now. Too old for bar stools. Too old for any kind of revenge. (RAMONA sits with back to audience. BEVERLY faces the other way. NIA and SHAQUILLE on the stairs at BEVERLY's house).

NIA: Are we really home Mama—cuz if need be i can go and be with my boyfriend's family. He lives over here in West Philadelphia. You can take care of Shaquille. i'll be all right. i know how to take care of myself.

SHAQUILLE: Nia's got a boyfriend. They always in each other's face. Laughing. Kissing 'n' stuff.

NIA: Oh shut up Shaquille. You don't know nothing.

BEVERLY: You can have my room Nia. Shaquille you'll sleep with Jamal. i have a couch in the basement. We'll figure this all out. Now go upstairs and put your things away. i left some space for your things. Tomorrow we'll go shopping for a few things. Shaquille you still like chicken? Nia you still a vegetarian?

SHAQUILLE: No more Mama. She eats more chicken than i do. *(Laughs)* *(They go upstairs.)*

BEVERLY: *(Begins to cry—then straightens up walks around her chair—comes back and sits)* i haven't spoken to you in a long time God. i'm not sure i believe in you anymore. Not since you took George away. He just died sitting on the toilet and that seemed like such a cruel way to take him. . . . We haven't talked in a long time but i got to talk to you today. i think i got to acknowledge that i need your help with these children. Half-grown and little at the same time. Hiding scars that i can't even see. And my money won't stretch to take care of two houses. What am i gonna do? Abandon my daughter again in that rundown place. And she so thin you could thread a needle with her. But i need to keep the money for these three children. They need things and food and clothes and self-respect—above all a little peace and privacy. They need me and the little money i got. Help me to be strong when she calls hurting in the night. Help me to remember Jamal's smile and smartness; help me to remember Nia's eyes asking for a safe harbor; help me to hold little Shaquille in the night when he screams out against his dreams. Help me to understand that it's because i love her that i help her children to live. Help me to listen to her then tell her that she needs to go for help. Help me to hang up on her when she screams obscenities and even when she starts to call me Mommie in that little used-to-be-sweet voice. . . . O make me strong when she comes round and bangs on the door. Hold me hard against her tears. Curses. Screams. Help me through these days and perhaps i'll forgive you for taking

George away that morning. i'll forgive you for that loneliness you spilled on my doorstep.

RAMONA: *(Stands and begins to circle BEVERLY—calling)* Mommie, Mommie—it's me. 'Mona—open the door. it's cold out here now. Don't have no coat. No food. Just let me come in for a little while—so i can sit and get some food. You're right; i'll go for treatment after tonight. Just let me stay here for tonight. See the children. Mommie it's me. 'Mona—help me Mommie— Mommie—got no place to go. We had a fire at the house. Mommie please help me; can't continue like this. Mommie.

RAMONA: *(Sits down—turns chair to audience)* i needed to be wild against the death patrolling my legs here in North Philadelphia. Can't you see Mama. i needed to come up against stuff. i needed to strut my stuff outside so no one would notice me—look my way—touch me—cuz they knew i was doing something against this silence—this deafening silence that surrounded us all. So the dope dealers left me alone—said, right on young sister—and when i stopped moving against the silence because of that look of fear in your eyes, because of your mouth demanding that i keep quiet and just be a good student, when i stopped and just walked without that protection, they knew. They began to notice my eyes with no hope or light in them—They began to notice my breasts, my hips, my big legs and they picked at them with words like—hey baby—hey lil sis—you busy? Want some of this stuff—make you feel/so/ good—hey there baby. What you up to here? You still in that school up there on the hill asking them white people for help? *(Laughs)* i got some authentic bonafide help for you right here. it'll make you feel good—make you forget what you wanna forget—That's right, c'mon over here to new memory—no caring about school or mothers or fathers—nobody. Just caring about you yourself and no one else. That's right c'mon over here and forget that pain in your eyes. All it costs is ten dollars—ten dollars for new memory in an old neighborhood. . . . And i went Mama, coming home from school where i sat silently in class and never heard my name over names spoken—when i heard teachers despise us with their indifferent tongues—they knew the education was a sham at that school. We were all just making time til June came. So i gave up learning/loving Langston Hughes and W.E.B. DuBois and

Malcolm and Harriet Tubman—They still spoke to me out of the corner of their mouths but i erased them finally with the Crack, that cracked my body during that last year in school. And you didn't even see it Mama. You were so happy that i was quiet. A good student. . . . *(Stops. Sits down in chair facing her mother)* Like you didn't even know that i remembered you leaving me in Baltimore—ah—you looking at me now Mama. Yes, i remembered you leaving me—depositing me with Aunt Beatrice—who didn't want to be bothered with no 6 yr. old child. i remember calling for you Mama—i called Mommy, Mommy, Mommy don't leave me. . . . Mommy, Mommy, Mommy come back. . . .Mommy, Mommy, Mommy. . . . Did i remember? i cried for days for you Mama—i called for you in my sleep—i cried as i watched TV with Aunt Beatrice—i cried with my eyes wide open—i stood at the screen door every-day looking for you and i wet my panties—along with my tears. *(Stands up—circles Mama) (Begins to touch her—sings in a sing-song fashion)* O Mommie, Mommie, Mommie, you came back for me—you here. . . . O Mommie i missed you so much O Mommie hold me—love me—You all i got—don't leave me Mommie. *(Puts head in Mama's lap—becomes a little girl again)* Mommie don't leave me. Mommie it's Ramona—i can't take care of myself. *(Mama touches RAMONA's head—caresses her— begins to sing)*

MAMA: Good morning to you
And how do you do
The trees they are blowing
We know that it's you. . . . .

RAMONA: O Mommie—i used to love that song—You sang it to me every day when i was little—*(begins to sing)*

Good morning to you
And how do you do
The trees they are blowing
We know that it's you. . . .

(They begin to sing the song together.)

RAMONA: *(Raises her head)* Remember Mama. i was valedictorian at graduation. Remember how proud you were Mama—You sat there with that funny looking hat on your head like you were all dressed up for church. And you clapped so hard when i finished my speech—Remember—i still remember the speech—ain't that funny—i still remember that i stood on stage and delivered it and everyone clapped at the end—especially you Mama. You stood up for me, clapped, because i was valedictorian at my H.S. graduation. *(Stands up)* Remember Mama—remember I said. . . *(RAMONA begins a dance of seduction around her mother—she climbs.)* Mommie look it's me 'Mona—here's my Spanish medal for excellence—here's my French medal for excellence—remember—Moma remember i was valedictorian at my high school—Moma look at me giving my speech.

(Goes to the coat rack and takes graduation hat and begins to speak)

To: Principal James Alterhurst, Vice Principal Jane Cleeves, our distinguished teachers and of course to our distinguished graduates. Well we made it. Right here in North Philadelphia. We made it because we realize that education is the key to everything. The great Philadelphian Benjamin Franklin wrote: "Education begins with life. Before we are aware the foundations of character are laid, and subsequent teaching avails but little to remove or alter them. If a man empties his purse into his head, no man can take it away from him. An investment in Knowledge always pays the best interest." And you know we are all interested in this kind of "interest" as we go out into this great world just waiting for us. So i say go out. The city awaits you. A job or college awaits you. Go out and be all that you can be. i want to end by quoting a great writer, Ralph W. Emerson, who wrote: "The secret of education lies in respecting the pupil." i could not agree more. Good luck. Hang loose. Know that we have done something here today. . . . Remember Mommie. They gave me a standing ovation and i just laughed and laughed so hard that you thought i was going to break a blood vessel. i laughed so hard after that speech that i almost peed on myself. i mean—*(she begins to laugh)*—i mean Mommie—*(laughs)*—I was thinking the whole time who's educating us? Who's leading us out of this darkness? *(Laughs)* i wanted to say who's leading us out of this darkness—this Philadelphia darkness—and we were still blindfolded and throwing our hats in the air—*(Laughs—*

becomes hysterical—falls on the floor and rolls with laughter—she can't stop—begins to call Mommie, Mommie in a very sad fashion—between laughs. Continues to laugh.) **Mommie, Mommie, Mommie.** . . . *(laughs again—a very hard laugh)*

BEVERLY: *(Stands up—pulls the chair to the back of the stage—begins to climb the stairs without looking back. RAMONA rolls on the floor, laughing and saying "Mommie." She can't catch her breath and begins to cough and laugh until she's still.)*

Selected Bibliography

Baldwin, James. "Theatre: The Negro In and Out." *Negro Digest*, April 1966, 37–44.

Baraka, Amiri (LeRoi Jones). "American Sexual Reference: Black Male." *Home: Social Essays*, 216–33. New York: William Morrow, 1966.

———. "AM/TRAK." *The LeRoi Jones/Amiri Baraka Reader*, edited by William J. Harris, 267–72. New York: Thunder's Mouth Press, 2000.

———. "Black Writing." *Home: Social Essays*, 161–65. New York: William Morrow, 1966.

———. *Blues People: Negro Music in White America*. 1963. Reprint, New York: William Morrow, 1999.

———. *Dutchman* and *The Slave*. New York: William Morrow, 1964.

———. "The Revolutionary Theatre." *Home: Social Essays*, 210–15. New York: William Morrow, 1966.

Barnes, Clive. "Black Visions." *New York Times*, April 5, 1972, sec. 37, 1.

Benston, Kimberly W. "The Aesthetic of Modern Black Drama: From *Mimesis* to *Methexis*." *The Theatre of Black Americans: A Collection of Critical Essays*, edited by Errol Hill, 61–78. 2nd ed. New York: Applause Theatre Book Publishers, 1990.

Bigsby, C. W. E. "The Theatre and the Coming Revolution." *Conversations with Amiri Baraka*, edited by Charles Reilly, 130–45. Jackson: University Press of Mississippi, 1994.

Brown-Guillory, Elizabeth. *Wines in the Wilderness: Plays by African American Women from the Harlem Renaissance to the Present*. New York: Praeger, 1990.

Bullins, Ed, ed. *The New Lafayette Theatre Presents*. Garden City, N.Y.: Anchor Press, 1974.

———, ed. *New Plays from the Black Theater*. New York: Bantam Books, 1969.

———. "Theatre of Reality." *Negro Digest*, April 1966, 60–66.

Carmichael, Stokely. "Black Power." *Black Protest: History, Documents, and Analyses, 1619 to the Present*, edited by Joanne Grant, 459–66. Greenwich, Conn.: Fawcett Publications, 1970.

———. *Stokely Speaks: Black Power Back to Pan-Africanism*. New York: Vintage Books, 1971.

Carmichael, Stokely, and Charles Hamilton. *Black Power: The Politics of Liberation in America*. New York: Random House, 1967.

Davis, Arthur, and Saunders Redding, eds. *Cavalcade*. Boston: Houghton Mifflin, 1971.

Du Bois, W. E. B. "Krigwa Players Little Negro Theatre." *The Crisis* 32 (1926): 134.

Elam, Harry J. Jr., and David Krasner, eds. *African American Performance and Theater History: A Critical Reader*. New York: Oxford University Press, 2001.

Evans, Mari, ed. *Black Women Writers*. New York: Anchor Books, 1984.

Fanon, Franz. *Black Skin, White Masks*. Translated by Charles Lam Markmann. New York: Grove Weidenfield Press, 1967.

———. *A Dying Colonialism*. Translated by Haakon Chevalier. New York: Grove Press, 1965.

———. *The Wretched of the Earth*. Translated by Constance Farrington. New York: Grove Press, 1963.

Fisher, Dexter, and Robert Stepto, eds. *Afro-American Literature: The Reconstruction of Instruction*. New York: Modern Language Association, 1978.

Gates, Henry Louis, ed. *Reading Black, Reading Feminist: A Critical Anthology*. New York: Meridian, 1990.

Gordon, Lewis R., T. Denean Sharpley-Whiting, and Renée White, eds. "Introduction: Five Stages of Fanon Studies," *Fanon: A Critical Reader*, 1–8. Cambridge, Mass.: Blackwell Publishers, 1996.

Hatch, James V. "Appendix: Theatre Scholarship 2002." *A History of African American Theatre*, edited by Erroll G. Hill and James V. Hatch, 482–87. Cambridge: Cambridge University Press, 2003.

———. "Some African Influences on the Afro-American Theatre." *The Theatre of Black Americans: A Collection of Critical Essays*, edited by Erroll G. Hill, 13–29. New York: Applause, 1990.

Hay, Samuel. *African American Theatre: A Historical and Critical Analysis*. New York: Cambridge University Press, 1994.

Henderson, Stephen, ed. *Understanding the New Black Poetry: Black Speech and Black Music as Poetic References*. New York: William Morrow, 1973.

Hill, Errol G., ed. *The Theatre of Black Americans: A Collection of Critical Essays*. New York: Applause, 1990.

Hill, Errol G., and James V. Hatch, eds. *A History of African American Theatre*. New York: Cambridge University Press, 2003.

Hilliard, David, and Donald Weise, eds. *The Huey P. Newton Reader*. New York: Seven Stories Press, 2002.

Hine, Darlene Clark, Elsa Barkley Brown, and Rosalyn Terborg-Penn, eds. *Black Women in America: An Historical Encyclopedia*. 2 vols. Bloomington: Indiana University Press, 1994.

Jackson, Ronald L. II, and Elaine B. Richardson, eds. *Understanding African*

American Rhetoric: Classical Origins to Contemporary Innovations. New York: Routledge, 2003.

Joyce, Joyce Ann. *Ijala: Sonia Sanchez and the African Poetic Tradition.* Chicago: Third World Press, 1996.

Kalem, T. E. "Black on Black." *Time,* May 1, 1972, 53.

Kennedy, Adrienne. *Funnyhouse of a Negro: In One Act.* Minneapolis: University of Minnesota Press, 1991.

———. *The Owl Answers: In One Act.* Minneapolis: University of Minnesota Press, 1991.

Kerr, Walter. "Gloria Is the Glory." *New York Times,* March 26, 1972, 11, 3, 1.

Klarman, Michael J. *From Jim Crow to Civil Rights: The Supreme Court and the Struggle for Racial Equality.* New York: Oxford University Press, 2004.

Kluger, Richard. *Simple Justice: The History of Brown v. Board of Education and Black America's Struggle for Equality.* Vol. 1. New York: Alfred A. Knopf, 1975.

Kroll, Jack. "What's Happening." *Newsweek,* April 17, 1972, 91–93.

Madhubuti, Haki (Don L. Lee). "Don't Cry, Scream." *Understanding the New Black Poetry: Black Speech & Black Music as Poetic References,* edited by Stephen Henderson, 336–43. New York: William Morrow, 1973.

———. "Sonia Sanchez: The Bringer of Memories." *Black Women Writers,* edited by Mari Evans, 419–32. New York: Anchor Books, 1984.

Maultsby, Paula K. "Africanisms in African-American Music." *Africanisms in American Culture,* edited by Joseph Holloway, 185–210. Bloomington: Indiana University Press, 1990.

McCauley, Robbie. *Sally's Rape. Black Theatre U.S.A.: Plays by African Americans—The Recent Period, 1935–Today,* edited by James V. Hatch and Ted Shine. New York: Free Press, 1996.

McElroy, Hilda. "In 'Uh, Uh; But How Do It Free Us,' Sanchez Flashes Scenes on Stage." *Black World,* April 1975, 80–83.

Meier, August, Elliot Rudwick, and Francis L. Broderick, eds. *Black Protest Thought in the Twentieth Century.* 2nd ed. New York: Macmillan, 1971.

Milner, Ron. "Black Theater Go Home!" *The Black Aesthetic,* edited by Addison Gayle Jr., 306–12. Garden City, N.Y.: Doubleday, 1971.

Neal, Larry. "The Black Arts Movement." *Drama Review* 12, no. 4 (Summer 1968): 29–39.

Newton, Huey P. "The Founding of the Black Panther Party." *The Huey P. Newton Reader,* edited by David Hilliard and Donald Weise, 49–52. New York: Seven Stories Press, 2002.

———. "Huey Newton Talks to the Movement." *Black Protest Thought in the Twentieth Century,* edited by August Meier, Elliot Rudwick, and Francis L. Broderick, 495–515. 2nd ed. New York: Macmillan, 1971.

———. "Intercommunalism: February 1971." *The Huey P. Newton Reader*, 181–99.

Parks, Suzan-Lori. *The Death of the Last Black Man in the Whole Entire World*. *The America Play and Other Works*, 99–131. New York: Theatre Communications Group, 1995.

———. *Imperceptible Mutabilities of the Third Kingdom*. *The America Play and Other Works*, 23–71. New York: Theatre Communications Group, 1995.

———. *Topdog, Underdog*. New York: Theatre Communications Group, 2001.

Reid, Margaret. *Black Protest Poetry: Polemics from the Harlem Renaissance and the Sixties*. New York: Peter Lang, 2001.

Roland, Paul, ed. *Jazz Singers: The Great Song Stylists in Their Own Words*. New York: Billboard Books, 2000.

Sanchez, Sonia. Personal interview. Alabama Writers' Symposium, May 5, 2004.

———. Personal interview. March 2005.

———. *Blues Book for Blue Black Magical Women*. Detroit: Broadside Press, 1974.

———. *Homecoming*. Detroit: Broadside Press, 1969.

———. *Homegirls and Handgrenades*. New York: Thunder's Mouth Press, 1984.

———. *I've Been a Woman*. Chicago: Third World Press, 1978.

———. *Love Poems*. New York: Third Press, 1973.

———. *Under a Soprano Sky*. Trenton, N.J.: Africa World Press, 1987.

———. *We a BaddDDD People*. Detroit: Broadside Press, 1970.

Shange, Ntozake. *boogie woogie landscapes: Three Pieces*. 1981. Reprint, New York: Penguin Books, 1992.

———. *for colored girls who have considered suicide/when the rainbow is enuf*. 1977. Reprint, New York: Samuel French, 1981.

———. "Program Note." *See No Evil: Prefaces, Essays and Accounts, 1976–1983*, 21–25. San Francisco: Momo Press, 1984.

Shevill, James, ed. *Breakout: In Search of New Theatrical Environments*. Chicago: Swallow Press, 1973.

Smith, Helene C. "Emotional Play Explores the Exploitation of Black Women." The *Atlanta Constitution*, April 30, 1982, sec. B, 1.

———. "Joy and Pain of Writing the Blues." The *Atlanta Constitution*, April 30, 1982, sec. 4.

"U.S. Lynchings by Race and by Year." Tuskegee Institute. Facts on File. *African-American History and Culture*. http://www.factsonfile.com.

Watts, Richard. "Four Plays by Black Authors." *New York Post*, April 5, 1972, 67.

Williams, David. "The Poetry of Sonia Sanchez." *Black Women Writers*, edited by Mari Evans, 433–48. New York: Anchor Books, 1984.

Williams, Mance. *Black Theatre in the 1960s and 1970s*. Westport, Conn.: Greenwood Press, 1985.

Williams, Sherley Anne. "The Blues Roots of Contemporary Afro-American Poetry." *Afro-American Literature: The Reconstruction of Instruction*, edited by Dexter Fisher and Robert Stepto, 72–87. New York: Modern Language Association, 1978.

Wood, Jacqueline. "'This Thing Called Playwriting': An Interview with Sonia Sanchez on the Art of Her Drama." *African American Review* 39 (2005): 119–32.

Woodward, C. Vann. *The Strange Career of Jim Crow*. 1955. Reprint, New York: Oxford University Press, 1966.

Sonia Sanchez is a playwright and poet. She is the author of *Conversations with Sonia Sanchez* (2007); *Shake Loose My Skin: New and Selected Poems* (1999); *Like the Singing Coming off the Drums: Love Poems* (1998); *Does Your House Have Lions?* (1997); *Wounded in the House of a Friend* (1995); *Under a Soprano Sky* (1987); *Homegirls and Handgrenades* (1984); *I've Been a Woman: New and Selected Poems* (1980); *A Blues Book for Blue Black Magical Women* (1974); *Love Poems* (1973); *The Adventures of Fathead, Smallhead, and Squarehead by Sonia Sanchez* (1973); *It's a New Day: Poems for Young Brothas and Sistuhs* (1971); *We Be BaddDDD People* (1970); and *Homecoming* (1969). She is the recipient of a PEN Writers Award.

Jacqueline Wood is an associate professor of African American literature and the interim director of the African American studies program at the University of Alabama, Birmingham.

Library of Congress Cataloging-in-Publication Data
Sanchez, Sonia, 1934–
I'm Black when I'm singing, I'm blue when I ain't and other plays / Sonia Sanchez ; edited and with an introduction by Jacqueline Wood.
p. cm.
Includes bibliographical references.
ISBN 978-0-8223-4757-6 (cloth : alk. paper)
ISBN 978-0-8223-4778-1 (pbk. : alk. paper)
1. African American women dramatists. 2. American drama—African American authors. 3. American drama—Women authors. 4. Black Arts movement. 5. American drama—20th century. I. Wood, Jacqueline. II. Title.
PS3569.A4681445 2010
812'.54080928708996073—dc22
2010009124